THE REAPPEARING ACT

Coming Out as Gay on a College Basketball Team Led by Born-Again Christians

KATE FAGAN

Skyhorse Publishing

All Rights Reserved. No part of this book may be reproduced in any manner without the express written consent of the publisher, except in the case of brief excerpts in critical reviews or articles. All inquiries should be addressed to Skyhorse Publishing, 307 West 36th Street, 11th Floor, New York, NY 10018.

Skyhorse Publishing books may be purchased in bulk at special discounts for sales promotion, corporate gifts, fund-raising, or educational purposes. Special editions can also be created to specifications. For details, contact the Special Sales Department, Skyhorse Publishing, 307 West 36th Street, 11th Floor, New York, NY 10018 or info@skyhorsepublishing.com.

Skyhorse® and Skyhorse Publishing® are registered trademarks of Skyhorse Publishing, Inc.®, a Delaware corporation.

www.skyhorsepublishing.com

10 9 8 7 6 5 4 3 2 1

Library of Congress Cataloging-in-Publication Data is available on file.

Cover design by Nim Ben-Reuven

ISBN: 978-1-62914-205-0
E-book ISBN: 978-1-62914-301-9

Printed in the United States of America

CONTENTS

Author's Note

I relied mainly on my own memory, journals, and notes while writing this memoir, although I did consult others, gathering their recollections, for certain sections. I have changed most, but not all, of the names of the individuals who appear in this book, in order to provide a level of anonymity. Occasionally, I also altered specific identifying details, but only when it seemed fair and appropriate to do so, and when it had no impact whatsoever on the substance of the story.

CHAPTER 1

March Madness

I sat in my car outside the arena, the vents releasing their last breaths of heated air. I closed my eyes for a moment and felt the nerves radiating through my body, my chest rising and falling as I deliberately filled my lungs, then slowly exhaled. My hands were trembling. I stared at them, concentrating, trying to still the movement. A minute or two passed, long enough that the inside of the car turned cold, my breaths like little clouds.

Then I gave up. My hands still shaking, I grabbed my backpack from the passenger's seat and slung it over my shoulder as I stepped out of the car and headed toward the arena. On the short walk to the players' entrance, I passed a large TV truck parked at the mouth of the Coors Events Center. My teeth began chattering, and I gritted them, the energy spreading to my jawline, making it vibrate. I pulled open the door and nodded hello to Ron the usher, the same usher who had greeted me at every home game I had ever played for the University of Colorado. "Big one," he said, and I glanced at the large ESPN banner hanging on the wall over his shoulder. "It is," I replied, giving him a high five, just as I had done dozens of times before. Could he sense my nerves? I tried to swallow them.

I turned right and walked down the hallway, stopping to poke my head inside the training room to say hello to Kristen, our head trainer, who was sitting behind her computer. "In here whenever you need me," she said, her tone more serious than usual, because tonight really was a big deal. I nodded and said thanks. The locker room for the women's basketball team was only a few steps past the training room. The wooden door was closed; I was the first player to arrive. I walked in and glanced at the black couch to the left of the door, its leather cracked and wrinkled. I had napped on that couch a hundred times, in the long afternoons before late practices. I had even slept there all night once, just a few weeks earlier, when I couldn't stand the thought of tossing and turning, yet again, in my own bed. I had the urge to curl up on that couch now, hug my backpack to my chest, and close my eyes for a while.

Instead, I sat on my stool—the one with my name written on it in cursive—and faced my closed locker. Our director of basketball operations had already hung our uniforms on the outsides of our lockers. I looked at mine, crisp and white, with "Colorado" written in black across the chest, just above my number: 1. How many times, in previous years, had I walked into this arena knowing that I would play only sparingly? A year earlier, during my sophomore season, I had sat on the bench inside Boise State's arena and watched as our seniors, some of my best friends in the world—the same friends whose support I was now about to lose—led us to victory over Stanford and a berth in the Elite Eight of the NCAA tournament. For years, I had waited for a moment like tonight. I would start and play most of the game, as I had done all season. But tonight's game was more important than all the rest, the culmination of everything before it. Tonight, we were playing the North Carolina Tar Heels in the second round of the 2003 NCAA tourney, televised on ESPN.

And I couldn't even fucking concentrate. I chucked my backpack into my locker and looked down at my hands again, then started rubbing them together, as if warming them by a fire. I sat like that for a while, competing thoughts swirling in my mind, until the first of my teammates arrived. "Hey you," said Jamie, our starting power forward. I turned toward her as she was taking off her coat and hanging it in her locker, and I realized I was still wearing my own jacket. I stood and started executing the first item on my pregame list, undressing and putting on my uniform.

Two hours later, the stands were filled with six thousand people. Beads of sweat dripped across my eyebrows, and I kept wiping them away. I looked at the referee, who was holding the game ball and watching the official scorer, waiting for ESPN to signal a return from commercial. I pretended to glance at the scoreboard, but really I was looking into the stands, high up in the corner, for someone who wasn't there. The referee blew the whistle signaling we were ready, then walked to center court, the ball resting on her palm as if on a tray. I arranged my feet around the jump circle, something I had done a thousand times in my life.

But this time was different. Because this time, as the ball flew into the air for the opening tip, I wasn't thinking about tracking it down while fighting for position with the player next to me. I wasn't even thinking about basketball. In that moment, my mind was focused on one thing in particular.

Holy shit . . . I'm definitely gay.

CHAPTER 2

The Hot Cuts Experiment

My mother, Kathy, offered her children the freedom of choice that her own mother had not. Her mother insisted she eat everything on her plate, regardless of taste preference, and forced her to drink all her cereal milk, including the discolored warm leftovers at the bottom of the bowl. These may seem like harmless edicts, but over the years I gathered they were only a microcosm, and that choking down broccoli was among the more trivial events of my mother's mildly traumatic childhood, which included a constant fear of judgment from my shockingly self-absorbed grandmother and many sleepless nights waiting for my irritable grandfather to stumble home from the local bar.

Once she became a parent, my mom vowed free choice for her two daughters. For me, this meant I could eat my broccoli or I could not. (I chose not.) I could wear my favorite McGraw Hill navy sweatshirt to school two weeks in a row if I so desired. (I did.) And, in what would become one of my childhood's most defining moments, I could cut my hair in any style I wanted. At the time, this last choice sounded fantastic. But I would soon learn that while certain decisions might be mine to make, the right to judge them remained everyone else's, especially the person giving me the freedom—especially my mother.

My life, or more precisely, how I perceived life, changed when I was eight years old. I wanted to wear my hair like my Little League teammates did. They were all boys. Baseball season had just begun, and I was in Double-A, which meant we were no longer using a tee. We didn't have fathers pitching, either. In my eight-year-old mind, this was big-time baseball. My team was the Golden Glovers; we wore black t-shirts and caps. I could field just like the boys and hit just like the boys. But unlike the boys, I had to constantly shove my curly mop under my cap. Every few minutes, I was tucking loose strands back out of the way, out of sight.

I didn't want to be different, and that's why I found myself inside Mohawk Mall with my mother one spring weekend. With its tan carpet, brick walls, and dim lighting, the one-level shopping center—located in our upstate New York town of Niskayuna, a suburb of Schenectady—had the feel of a remodeled prison. (This consumer penitentiary was bulldozed before I graduated high school.) We had just walked through the front entrance, and Hot Cuts was the first storefront on the right. Not that I have to point this out, because salons like Hot Cuts always seem to be in the same spot, calling out like a siren's song to the shaggy-haired masses. There was a tacky water feature, encased by a brick circle, in front of the salon, and we stood there, having arrived a few minutes early for my appointment. Mom's black purse was tucked under her arm, her heels only inches from the brick. I faced her, like a miniature version, and crossed my arms. I tucked my chin and looked down at the thin, dirty carpet.

"Honey, are you nervous?" she asked.

I kept my eyes down and shook my head in some sort of non-committal manner. Maybe, maybe not, I hoped the gesture would convey. But of course I was nervous! I was about to sit in a chair in front of some stranger holding a pair of scissors. And this person was going to depend on my instructions—and mine alone—to execute my haircut. The thought of this one-on-one communication frightened me far more than the scissors.

"Do you know what kind of haircut you want to get?" My mom seemed genuinely interested in my answer. I would learn years later that she despised her own hair—curly and coarse, by her estimation—while envying the texture of mine. My father had thin, straight hair, and in my mother's opinion, I was the world's luckiest girl because my hair was a genetic cross of theirs.

"Something good for baseball," I said with a shrug. That was really my most pressing concern. I was going to ask my hairstylist to cut it really short so I looked like all my teammates—no curls sticking out from beneath my cap. I wanted a close cut, perfect for taking off my cap and sliding on a batting helmet without causing a big production.

Mom flinched, like I had kicked her in the shins. Eventually, by the time I was a teenager, I could instantly translate that kind of reaction: *You're going to do what*?! But I wasn't yet fluid in the language of my mother.

"It's your decision, Katie," she said as she began rummaging through her purse, eyes scanning the contents. We stood there without speaking for another minute or two before she glanced at her thin, gold wrist watch and announced it was time for my appointment. We walked the few steps to the front counter of Hot Cuts. Mom did the initial talking for me—*appointment, my daughter, shampoo and cut, first time*—and then waved goodbye while a woman ushered me to the sink basins along the salon's back wall. When I lifted my clean, sopping head from the sink, my mother was gone.

There was no internal rebellion as I told the hairstylist how to cut my hair. I simply tugged at the curly mess on the sides and back and shook my head like this was tragic.

"Can you cut it off?" I asked. "Can you make it as short as you can?"

The woman squinted her eyes and then glanced to the space where my mother had stood. "Yeah?" She tilted her head and smacked her gum.

This should have been a clue. If today I entered a hair salon, explained my desired cut, and received a similar response from the stylist—narrowed eyes, tilted head, and a "Yeah?" that sounded very similar to "For real?"—I'd probably throw on the brakes and reevaluate. But there's such freedom in being eight, such simplicity. The hairstylist and I were both facing forward, and I watched her reflection in the mirror, then nodded my head a couple of times to reassure her. "Yup," I said. "It's for baseball this summer."

There was a slight pause before she leaned forward and removed her scissors from a jar of blue liquid. I had no inkling how shaping my hair would shape my life. I didn't hold my breath or worry that she was cutting off too much. There was no such thing as cutting off too much—at least not in that moment. It took her about fifteen minutes to create my new look, and as each tuft of unruly hair fell to the floor, I became increasingly sure that I had done exactly the right thing. She returned the scissors to the blue liquid and grabbed what looked like a badminton shuttlecock, with bristles at the end. She held the knob in her hand and brushed off the back of my neck in a quick, tidy motion. Then she removed my cape in a flurry, as if she were a magician.

The grand reveal!

I stood and admired my new look, perfect for a ball cap. I enthusiastically thanked the woman, paid with the ten-dollar bill my mother had given me, and left Hot Cuts feeling light and free. Mom was waiting at the fountain, facing away from me, so I had the fun of surprising her. I walked to within a few feet, pausing until she sensed my arrival. She turned, and in that initial moment, her face appeared open and expressionless. But then she drew a sharp breath and raised her right hand, quickly, to the space just below her throat. A look of pain flashed into her eyes, before she managed to blink it away.

"Mom," I said, taking a step forward. "Are you okay?"

She pasted a smile onto her lips and nodded vehemently. In retrospect, I can appreciate how hard she tried to shield me from her reaction, her emotions. She looked like she had something caught in her throat, like she couldn't get enough air. I peered up at her, confused more than worried. She put a hand on my shoulder and steered us toward the exit. I walked beside her through the parking lot until we reached her Ford Taurus, then slid into the passenger's seat and pulled the door shut. My mom did the same. But we didn't go anywhere. She didn't turn the key in the ignition or look over her shoulder so she could back out of the parking spot. Instead, she stared straight ahead, as if we were watching a movie at a drive-in theater.

I fidgeted in my seat, finally asking, "What's wrong?"

My mother, the woman I adored most in the world, began crying. She wasn't sobbing; her shoulders weren't heaving with effort. No, it was much more frightening than that. Water was simply escaping from her eyes.

"It's a boy's haircut," she said, turning over the engine.

Yes! I thought. It is a boy's haircut!

"But you're my beautiful daughter," she said, shifting the Taurus into reverse.

Oh. Oh no. I'd done something wrong. And it couldn't be undone.

I pulled down the visor and looked at my reflection in the small, square mirror. I touched the back of my neck, shocked at the absence of hair and the prickly feeling where the hairstylist had used an electric razor to even the cut.

"Are you upset at me, Mommy?"

"No, Mommy's just sad, that's all."

When I asked my mother that question, I had assumed the emotion of anger was the worst of all. But she swapped anger with sadness, which felt a little like switching a wooden baseball bat for metal; both were equally powerful. Until this moment, the things I'd done that usually upset her were avoidable, understandable— like eating a second cookie when she had said one was enough, or talking back when I didn't like her answer, or refusing to help with the chores. But this particular time, I couldn't clearly identify what exactly I had done wrong. I just knew something wasn't right.

I glanced through the driver's side window, at the mirror on the door, my reflection coming back to me at an angle. I tilted my head in the hope that this would improve the view. Maybe I did look too much like a boy. I had not yet learned that one of society's unwritten rules was that I was supposed to make it easy for everyone to identify my gender. Wearing my hair short under a baseball cap confused the hell out of people—restaurant waitresses, women in public restrooms. But it took a few years before my short hair confused me, too. Hot Cuts was my introduction to lingering disappointment. In seeking uniformity with my teammates, I had inadvertently ostracized myself. Bees began swarming in my stomach as I watched my mother quell her sadness. Those bees built a hive.

The lesson I learned that afternoon: Being who I am might make my loved ones cry.

CHAPTER 3

I QUIT

I did not want to play basketball anymore—could not stand another day of practice. And that's exactly what I was about to tell Ceal Barry, the head coach at Colorado, the woman who had believed in me enough to offer me a full scholarship. She was not the only coach to recruit me, but she was the only one whose program was consistently nationally ranked. When it came down to choosing which college to attend, I picked CU because I wanted to test myself at the highest level, playing for a coach who would win more than five hundred games in her career. And here I was, crumbling beneath the weight of it all after only a few weeks of official basketball practice.

I was still wearing my practice gear: black mesh shorts and a reversible mesh jersey. I had grabbed my sweatshirt from the cubicle inside the weight room and pulled it over my head. Coach Barry was walking in front of me, leading the way out, then snaking through the training room and into the empty office of an assistant trainer, who wasn't at work because it was Saturday. She flipped on the lights and lowered herself into a chair. My teammates and I had just lifted weights inside the Dal Ward Athletic Center, which overlooked the football stadium and offered, especially at dusk, an inspiring view of the Flatirons, the Boulder foothills leading to the crescendo of the Rocky Mountains. I stumbled my way through the lifting session, choking back tears, feeling broken, barely able to keep the dumbbells from crashing down and splitting my head open.

I slipped into the office with Coach Barry, but stood just inside the doorway, with my back covering the light switch, as if I couldn't fully commit to being there. At that moment, I didn't feel capable of committing to much of anything. Coach didn't seem to have any inkling of what I might say, but she was definitely aware of how pathetic I had been at practice lately. I closed the door behind us. She looked at me, expectantly.

"I just . . ." I glanced at her, then down at the tops of my sneakers. I told myself to look up again, to be mature. I met her gaze. "I think I'm going to have to quit," I said. "That's all. That's what I needed to say."

She leaned forward, closing the distance between us, and let out a long breath. My commitment to quitting was strong, but not ironclad. Although I was a sophomore academically, I was in my freshman season with the basketball team because I had spent the previous year on the injured list, after being granted a medical redshirt. I was diagnosed with a stress fracture in my right foot during the fall of 1999, before basketball practice even started, and I eventually had season-ending surgery that December, with the team doctor inserting a screw into the bone to keep it from fully breaking. As a result, I spent my first year at CU hanging out with my teammates and getting all the benefits of being a college athlete without having to do much of the serious training.

As I stood in front of Coach Barry that October day, I was healthy again, at least physically. I could run and jump and shoot; I just had zero motivation to do so. A week earlier, I had ingested an entire box of iron pills—my roommate and teammate, Dee, was anemic—in the hope that I would become violently ill and our trainer would be forced to excuse me from practice. I trudged down to the arena fully expecting to spend the afternoon hunched over the toilet. But, to my dismay, nothing happened. I felt fine. So I ended up having to practice, even less mentally prepared than usual.

I had convinced myself I didn't like basketball anymore. In fact, I took it one step further: I had *never* liked basketball. My father, Chris, was the one who loved the game; I was just mimicking him this entire time. And now that I was in the thick of it—hours and hours of mandatory practice, six days a week—I was being exposed as a fraud. The game was supposed to be in my blood, passed down to me through my dad, who starred at Colgate University and then spent several years playing professionally overseas, in places like Amsterdam and Corsica. My older sister, Ryan, was born in Corsica, in a tiny little hospital, which makes her a dual citizen, French and American. (I was born in Rhode Island—whatever.) Ryan ran track at Dartmouth, becoming an All-American her senior year. We had been raised to think sports were as nourishing as water, pursuing activities and developing team allegiances that we took very seriously. And I liked it that way, most of the time. Sports provided an always-open line of communication. There was sometimes little to say, but there was never nothing to say. I could always talk about the Mets, the Knicks, the Giants. Even if every other line was dangling, disconnected, the cable on which sports ran was always plugged in. And I would rely on that line for many years later in life.

I thought of my father as I watched Coach Barry lean forward, resting her elbows on her knees and dropping her head, clearly thinking about how to respond to my declaration. My dad had taught me how to shoot, spending countless hours practicing with me in the driveway and in the gym. And it was this skill—the ability to shoot well—that made me valuable to every team I played on. Because of his dedication, my dad had been disappointed when I chose Colorado, which was three-quarters of the way across the country from Schenectady. Why couldn't I have attended school closer to home? I know he viewed my choice as a slight to him; after everything we had done together, after all those hours and drills and shared Gatorades, he felt like I had decided I didn't need him anymore.

When I was a kid, Dad and I spent every Saturday morning together. He didn't need to wake me, or tell me what time we were leaving the house, or honk the car horn announcing our departure. I knew the schedule because Saturday morning was all about basketball.

"Leave in five?" Dad would say, dropping the *New York Times* to look at me. I'd quickly respond—*yes, sure, of course*—and scamper upstairs to my bedroom for my t-shirt, shorts, and basketball sneakers.

"You got the ball?" he'd ask, just before pushing through the front door. I'd pop into the front-hall closet, scoop up the worn men's basketball, then follow him outside, carrying my sneakers in one hand and the ball, which must have looked huge balancing on my small palm, in the other. Dad carried his basketball sneakers— wearing them outside was bad for the soles, he explained—so I did, too. We'd toss our stuff into the backseat of his blue Audi, then climb into the front and head for Stewart's, a convenience store about a mile away through the square blocks of our suburban neighborhood. A few minutes later, we'd pull into the parking lot.

"I buy, you fly?" Dad liked to say. I had probably already eaten a bowl (or two) of cereal for breakfast, but still I held out my hand for the money. "The *Post* and the *Daily News*, if they have them."

I nodded.

A minute later, I returned with some change in one hand, a raspberry swirled Danish in the other, and a couple of newspapers tucked under my arm. The change and the papers went to my dad; the Danish was mine. Perhaps at first, the food had been a bribe, his attempt to get me to enjoy reading newspapers while idling outside a convenience store. But later, the Danish became just another part of our ritual. I believe my participation in the reading and the idling were independent of this treat, but I can't be sure.

After I finished eating, which never took long, he handed me a newspaper. We'd start from the back page, the sports section, and turn toward the front.

"Big series this weekend," I would say, after reading that the Mets were only a few games out of first place.

"Things are lining up nicely," he might respond.

"They can do it," I'd say, full of hope.

"Wouldn't that be nice? But don't forget, they're the Mets."

We would read some more, staying maybe half an hour, until my fingertips were covered in newsprint and it was time for basketball. Then I'd put both papers at my feet and we'd drive to the gym.

So, yeah, my dad was disappointed when I chose to play college hoops on the other side of the country. He thought I had made a mistake, said it was too far from home, that I wouldn't have a support system. Now here I was proving him right.

"I think quitting is a mistake," Coach Barry said, lifting her head. She seemed about to say more, but paused, perhaps wanting to see how I would respond. I leaned into the wall and bounced my shoulders a few times, looking at the ceiling.

"My heart is just not in it," I said, and I could feel my eyes burning, the twisting of the faucet behind my tear ducts. "I'm scared to death of practice. It's the last place in the world I want to be. Nothing is going right."

This last part was true; I was playing terribly. Coming out of high school, I had thought I was so damn good. I was one of the better scholastic players in New York state, but now I couldn't even finish a drill without being told I had done it the wrong way and needed to do it over—and why was I so pathetic? (The last question was my own addition, the kind of destructive self-talk I gave into as I walked to the end of the line during drills.)

Coach Barry stood and took a step toward me. She half sat, half leaned on the desk, clasping her hands on her lap. "This is what we'll do," she said. "You'll give me two more weeks, and I'll change how I coach you. I think that's the problem here. Just give me two weeks."

My lack of perspective was frightening in that moment. To me, two weeks felt like an outrageous sentence handed down by an angry judge. We practiced six days a week in the preseason, sometimes twice a day. Two weeks meant twelve to fourteen practices, totaling about forty hours of basketball. And do you know how many drills can be packed into that amount of time?

I had no idea how to respond, so I didn't.

"Here's the thing," Coach Barry continued. "I think I misjudged how you need to be coached."

A tear rolled down my cheek, and I quickly wiped it away with the back of my sweatshirt. Coach put a frown on her face. It was a pitying look that seemed to say, *See? This is exactly what I mean.* And she was right. She didn't really get me yet, but I couldn't fault her that much. After all, I didn't get me, either. She would say later that she assumed I had a thick skin because I was stoic, that of all the current players she had recruited, she thought she'd be able to criticize me the most. Every coach needs a whipping girl, a player to make an example of, to teach the lessons intended for the rest of the team. In this way, college basketball is a lot like medieval punishment: *Behold this young woman in the stocks! This is what happens to anyone who misses a block-out!*

In those first months of college practice, Coach Barry had been breaking me down. And trust me, it didn't take her long. I understand her miscalculation, though. I had a dry sense of humor, I was from New York (not the city, but to people in Colorado, all of New York was a city), and I actively tried to give off the vibe that nothing bothered me, even though most criticism whipped through me like an arctic wind. I hadn't even thought that my souring on basketball had anything to do with Coach Barry—which is odd, considering some of the on-court interactions we had.

The week prior to my "quitting," I was chasing down the starting point guard in a defensive drill, and I couldn't get into position in time. So I fouled her, grabbing her from behind just as she was about to go up for a layup. This seemed like the best option, because the alternative was watching her score, which felt like giving up. "Stop! Stop! Stop!" Coach called out, walking from the sideline onto the middle of the court. She put her hands on her hips and stared at me, each second excruciating. "What the heck was that? First you're late getting back; then you commit a dangerous foul? So you didn't execute the drill, and you made it worse with a dumb play. What the heck are you thinking? Are you even thinking?" She let her words linger, looking at me as if waiting for a response. But of course I knew, as did everyone in the gym, that her questions were rhetorical and not an invitation to dialogue.

I stood on the baseline, surrounded by my teammates, who kept their eyes on Coach Barry and dared not look at me. I considered turning around, walking back to the locker room, collecting my things, and leaving—not just the arena, but the city of Boulder and the state of Colorado. I think I was even pivoting on my heel when Dee, my roommate, placed her hand on the small of my back and leaned over, the whole time keeping her eyes forward, as if Coach might be a bank robber and Dee needed to tell me to hit the panic button under the counter. "You're okay, Kate," she whispered, then drifted back to her standing position. I wanted to hug her, but of course I didn't. Coach Barry waved her hand in disgust, signaling the restarting of practice. I nodded to Dee, then walked to the end of the longest line, giving myself as much recovery time as possible before my next turn.

"I've been too hard on you." Coach Barry's words snapped me back to reality, to that little office in Dal Ward. She motioned toward the other chair in the room. I pushed myself away from the wall and shuffled forward. I was crying now, tears dripping down my cheeks faster than I could wipe them away. I noticed that the sleeve of my light gray Colorado sweatshirt was now stained wet. Coach laid out our game plan for the next two weeks. She would have our trainer schedule appointments for me with a sports psychologist. She would also revamp her approach to coaching me.

"You're way more sensitive than I imagined," she said, which made me roll my eyes and laugh—*Ya think?*—through my tears.

I accepted her terms. What choice did I have? Still, I wasn't particularly hopeful that a simple shift in coaching style, which seemed like a minor factor in my I Hate Basketball crisis, would make much of a difference. The day after my meeting with Coach Barry, I walked out to the court with Dee, who had supported my decision to quit even though it meant she would lose her closest friend on the team. She had proven herself an empathetic listener, and that made me like her even more.

"You ready for today?" Dee asked, as we each took a basketball off the rack and walked to a side hoop.

"I don't know," I said with a shrug. "What could possibly change? I just have to get through these two weeks." I dribbled until I was directly under the rim, then began the warm-up routine my dad had taught me. His words rang in my ears every time I stepped onto the court: *The best shooters never start from the three-point line; they gradually ease into the motion.*

"Maybe you'll be surprised," Dee said, lofting the ball off the backboard and in.

When practice started, I still had the same knot in my stomach—and dread is a burden when playing, like trying to run while wearing a weighted backpack. One of the first drills was a three-man weave down the court, returning in a two-on-one fast break, with the person who took the layup on the way down sprinting back as the lone defender. I started in the far right line, caught the pass from a teammate, and fired it across the court to the third member of our group. We bolted down the court and I ended up with the layup, banking it off the glass left-handed and quickly turning to race back on defense. At half-court, I spun around and began backpedaling, just as Coach Barry had taught us, so we had eyes on the offense as it attacked. My teammates passed the ball back and forth; then one of them took a dribble toward the rim, planted her foot, and reached for a layup. I slid under her, attempting to take the charge, and the two of us landed in a heap under the basket.

As we helped each other up, Coach Barry blew her whistle. The noise was short but intense, and translated to: *I have something to say about this.* I knew that I had been late in taking the charge. In a game, the referee would have called me for a blocking foul. So I held my breath and watched as Coach let the whistle drop from her mouth. "That's *exactly* the kind of effort we need more of," she said, making eye contact with the team. My brain scrambled to process the sentence; it seemed to be a compliment! "Kate has been busting it for weeks now," Coach continued. "And to tell you the truth, we could use more of the energy and effort she's been giving. Did everyone see how she backpedaled, got into position, and took that charge? That's what we need."

She stepped back to the sideline and yelled, "Next group up!" The only teammate who had any idea of what had just happened was Dee. I looked for her in the line next to mine. She caught my eye, and a hint of a smile crossed her lips. I made my eyes big for a split second, then turned forward as if nothing had happened. On my next turn, I tried even harder, wanting desperately to live up to the compliment, and came away with a deflection that ended the offensive attack. In the drill after that, feeling more confident than I had in months, I hit a three-pointer from the corner.

Over the next couple of weeks, Coach Barry built me into a mythological figure (in my own mind, at least). I became the team's unsung hero, a player whose effort and dedication on each possession would become the stuff of legend. I was like the Rudy of Colorado women's basketball. Multiple times, Coach singled out my performance in practice as the model for how things should be done. In this way, she carved out a little place for me on the team: I was Captain of the Backups, the second-string guard who cared little about her own lack of playing time while selflessly delivering maximum effort simply for the betterment of the squad. After two weeks, I was bouncing onto the court before practice, smiling and laughing and ready for another day of unsung hero awesomeness.

I loved my new role. No one ever criticized, no one ever disliked the unsung hero.

CHAPTER 4

COME TO JESUS

We were always praying. Like, all the time. And praying, I quickly came to understand, was done when the answer was complicated.

I didn't know that Jesus Christ had died for my sins. I mean, sure, I knew he was a really important guy—the son of God, no less—but when I arrived on Colorado's campus as a freshman, I could not have told you specifically what Jesus had done during his time on earth. My family was non-practicing Catholic, which meant that some years we attended church on Easter, and other years not at all. One time in high school, while I was stretching before cross-country practice, a teammate began talking to someone else about her faith and who Jesus was for her, but then I stood up to stretch my calves and didn't hear the rest of the conversation. Point is, when I got to Colorado, I literally did not know what I did not know—about Jesus, that is.

One night in the middle of my sophomore season (and junior academic year), I had just finished eating dinner with my teammates inside the athletes-only cafeteria located on the second floor of the Dal Ward complex, directly above the weight room. Sometimes during dinner, the building would vibrate when a hulking offensive lineman dropped his massive weight after a successful power clean. My teammates and I ate there five times a week, often gorging ourselves on foods like chicken fried steak and mashed potatoes with gravy. On this particular evening, I was standing by the ice cream freezer, elbow-deep in a tub of cookies 'n cream, when Sasha, our senior starting small forward, asked me if I wanted to join her and some of my teammates in the auditorium for "FCA."

"What's that?" I asked, as I plopped a heaping scoop of ice cream into my Styrofoam cup.

"It's this really cool fellowship group," Sasha said. "They hold it down in the football team's meeting room. There's a lot of singing and fellowship." She paused, then added, "Most of us are going— Dee, too."

Dee had become my best friend in the world. She and I were both from New York and had played on the same AAU summer team in high school. She could dunk a tennis ball and bench press twice as much weight as I could. She had calf muscles like softballs, smooth black skin, and beautiful almond eyes. I loved her incongruities. Dee's body was ripped, and yet she had the softest demeanor; she never got angry. Her idea of a good time was watching *The Golden Girls* or listening to Elvis Presley. She also had an ability I will never claim: she could laugh at herself. This made us a perfect pair as friends, because I'd poke fun at her and she'd burst into giggles. Even better, we also spent long hours discussing serious things like humanity's place in the universe, or whether Coach Barry regretted recruiting us. After two years of rooming together, we were tighter than ever.

I had never really given the term "fellowship" a second thought (I would eventually come to know it as the go-to buzzword for young Christians), but Sasha clearly understood that I'd be more willing to consider this invitation if I knew Dee was going.

"What's FCA stand for?" I asked, diving back into the ice cream for a second scoop.

"Fellowship of Christian Athletes," Sasha answered.

I tilted my head at her. Sasha was the strongest player on our team; she was stocky, built like the Toyota RAV4 that she drove, but she also possessed surprising finesse on the court, the combination making her difficult to guard. The two of us had never developed a particularly close friendship, mostly because she was a no-worries girl from California and I was a sarcastic New Yorker. In fact, most of our one-on-one interactions ended with Sasha wearing a puzzled look and me reassuring her that my words had been tongue-in-cheek.

Fellowship of Christian Athletes. Huh. I had no idea what these words, put into this order, actually meant in tangible terms. Today, if someone invited me to an FCA meeting, I would turn and run in the other direction. I would not, under any circumstances, want to sit in an auditorium and "worship" to Christian rock music, then listen to someone give testimony about how God works. But on that day, all I heard was that half of my teammates, Dee included, would be spending the evening at some sort of concert in the football team's meeting room. My boyfriend at the time, Derek, was away at medical school, so my social calendar was perpetually clear. If my teammates were going, I wanted to go.

"Sure," I told Sasha, fishing a plastic spoon out of the utensils container. "I'll go."

"Cool," she said, and I followed her back into the dining hall, toward the two round tables where members of our team were seated. "Kate's going," Sasha announced to the group at one table, which I then realized was filled entirely with the teammates who were attending FCA that night. There were seven of us, including me. Everyone stood and we began walking, heading for the basement of Dal Ward, toward the football team's meeting room, which I'd never actually been inside before.

I walked with Dee, side by side, our team-issued backpacks draped over our shoulders. I was digging into my ice cream, which was still rock-hard, when I asked her, "If you had to explain to me what's actually happening right now, could you?" I figured Dee would probably have a better understanding of these things than I, considering she was African-American and had grown up occasionally attending church. We had never discussed religion beyond sharing our basic family backgrounds, but I suppose I was employing the stereotype that black people have soul and tend to Believe with a capital B.

Dee: "Yeah, we're going to an FCA meeting, which is kind of like a low-key worship session."

Me: "And we're doing this voluntarily?"

She laughed and put her arm around my shoulder. "I think you're going to like it," she said.

We filed into the meeting room, which sloped downward and contained about twenty rows of plush chairs facing a small stage and a projection screen. It was inside this room that the football team watched film and met at halftime of games to talk strategy. I walked down a few steps and joined my teammates in their row. A man was standing at the front of the room, playing guitar, while a woman sang into a microphone. An old-fashioned projector beamed a page of text onto the screen:

> *Jesus, lover of my soul*
> *Jesus, I will never let You go*
> *You've taken me*
> *From the miry clay*
> *You've set my feet upon the rock*
> *And now I know*
> *I love You, I need You*
> *Though my world may fall, I'll never let You go*
> *My savior, my closest friend*
> *I will worship You until the very end*

I was busy looking into my Styrofoam cup, trying to see if the underside of my cookies 'n cream had melted enough for me to scrape off a substantial bite, when Dee put her hands on her knees and launched herself into standing position. She began clapping to the rhythm, swaying gently back and forth.

This was Day 1 of my new life as a Temporary Christian.

—ↄ—

In the weeks that followed, I attended FCA along with my teammates on Thursday nights. I would listen carefully, and then later, as we drove home, I'd ask Dee questions. *So people actually believe Jesus is their closest friend? And they believe everything in the Bible is the actual word of God? What about you? What do you believe?* Everything about FCA seemed fine, harmless even. I was learning about something that seemed important, something I was completely ignorant of: religious faith. I was absorbing the songs and the testimony, and talking with Dee about what we had heard.

And then one Thursday night, as we walked into the meeting room, we were given a handout. I sat down, placed my backpack at my feet, and glanced at the paper. "Overcoming Struggles of the Flesh," was the headline, written in bold. Underneath, in bullet point, was a list of the flesh's struggles: sex, alcohol, drugs, pride, homosexuality. I turned the sheet over and laid it by my feet. I took a deep breath, hoping the additional oxygen would help calm my heart. My cheeks felt hot, as if the eyes of everyone in the room were on me. I looked at Dee, but she was still reading the handout. I glanced diagonally at her sheet, reading the list of words a second time. Again my heart jumped, like a bungee cord being released, when I read the last word on the list. I found this reaction disturbing but told myself I shouldn't.

Those weekly FCA meetings began spilling over into the occasional Bible study, where we would pray about everything, especially whenever something became complicated. At one particular Bible session, my teammate Melissa, distraught over a recent knee injury that had sidelined her for the year, confessed that she was angry at God and felt abandoned by him. When Melissa said this, we all remained silent for what felt like a long time. There were six of us gathered around a coffee table: three on the couch, three sitting cross-legged on the carpet. Our Bibles were on the table in front of us, all open to the same verse. I racked my brain to come up with something godly to say to Melissa, something that would elevate my status within the group. I imagined everyone nodding at my advice—*Amen*—and Melissa being totally reassured and impressed. I ran through a couple of options, but then realized I was in way over my head on this one. I was the straggler of the group, the one least likely to volunteer to lead prayer, the one who would probably fall into the depths of Hell if any of my teammates looked the other way for too long. Someone else reached for her Bible, then began flipping through the pages purposefully. She was onto something—just give her a minute.

Then Chrissy, the FCA group leader who also ran the Bible study, sat forward and held hands with the girls on each side of her. "We should pray about this," she said. *Of course!* We linked hands and bowed our heads. "Heavenly father," Chrissy whispered, as if God had grabbed some popcorn and was leaning in. "We come before you humbled by your awesomeness. We are awed by you in every way. And, and . . . just thankful, God. Just so thankful. Tonight, we lift up Melissa to you, God."

At this point in the prayer, whoever was holding Melissa's hands probably squeezed them reassuringly. But we never actually addressed why Melissa might be feeling that way. We never let her vent about how unfair life could be. We never fully acknowledged what we all knew to be true, that a torn ACL and reconstructive surgery is a serious body blow for a competitive athlete. Everything was very simple. Whatever answers the Bible did not expressly offer—sadly, Jesus was silent on the topic of ACL injuries—were ones that should be sought through prayer.

I was a pretender in the Bible study. I told myself to be patient, that eventually faith would come, but I was never a true believer. I was just trying to do the thing that everyone always tells you to do: Fake it until you make it. Maybe someday, I'd tell myself, you will actually feel God's presence, his love.

Maybe someday.

CHAPTER 5

PRAY FOR COACH

I tried so hard to love Jesus in the way my Christian teammates told me they did, madly and deeply, as if he walked beside them, holding their hands and whispering advice at every turn. I bought myself a leather-bound Bible and read through it. Sometimes, my friends would quiz themselves to see who could name, in order, all of the books of the New Testament. It always reminded me of when my dad and I would try to name all fifteen players on the New York Knicks. We would inevitably forget one guy—always just one and always someone different from the previous time we went through the roster. My teammates, though, never missed a beat with the Bible, stringing the names of the books together like they were all one word: Matthewmarklukejohnactsromans . . .

This skill also helped them to find passages quickly. If Chrissy told us to turn to Ephesians 5:21 during Bible study, my teammates flipped to the correct page as if they had already dog-eared the passage. Meanwhile, I fumbled around in the back of the book, often having to lick my fingers and pretend like the pages were stuck together. I'd roll my eyes and give a look that said, "One more second! Circumstances out of my control here, people!"

At night, tucked away in my room, in the back corner of the one-floor apartment I shared with Dee and two other teammates, I would try to clear my mind and dive into the words that I was told came directly from God. But I couldn't connect with any of it, despite the façade I had adopted for the benefit of my friends—attending FCA and Bible studies with them, highlighting passages in my Bible, and writing notes to myself in the margins, such as "God loves each hair on my head." I even took my mother to dinner, when she was visiting Boulder, and tried to convert her. As the two of us chatted over Italian food at Buca di Beppo, I shared my passion for Jesus, telling her she should consider becoming a Christian. "You know, to cover all your bases," I explained, prompting her to reply, "Thanks, I'm all set," as she dipped a piece of bread into olive oil, then chewed it slowly while trying to signal our waiter for the check.

This busywork was done not to build my understanding of The Almighty, but rather so I would be deemed worthy enough to retain my membership in the group, because the leaders of the Christian movement on our team—seniors Sasha, Kelly, and Lisa—also made up three-fifths of our starting lineup. They were older and more talented, the cool kids. Sasha was from San Diego, the daughter of a female Lutheran minister, but she had held her faith close to the vest during her first two years at Colorado, reading her Bible late at night and rarely talking about her beliefs with any of us. That changed when she moved in with Kelly and Lisa for their junior season. Kelly and Lisa, a pair of Colorado natives, had played on the same AAU team in high school, then became a tag-team in college. Kelly was a speedy shooting guard with a smooth jumper; Lisa was an imposing center with a deft touch near the rim. Both came from faith-based families, but they didn't recommit themselves to Jesus until teaming up with Sasha. I was in awe of all of them my first two years in Boulder. Kelly was the best player I'd ever seen, so sure of herself on the court. Lisa was sharp, with a great sense of humor, and I took it as a personal challenge to make her laugh, to try to match wits. When the three of them gravitated toward Jesus, they pulled everyone in their orbit, including me, along with them, toward their sun.

But the only time anything in the Bible made sense to me was when Dee and I went for rides in "Ernie," the nickname she gave to her gray Jeep Cherokee. We would often drive through the Colorado plains at dusk, with the glowing outline of the Flatirons visible in the distance. It was in these moments, as Dee burned with excitement about her burgeoning faith, that I most connected with the idea of a higher power. The car was warm and my friend's voice was hot with hope and passion. She had found her path. So I tried to see what she saw.

At that point during my time as a temporary Christian, I was on cruise control. I was a valued member of the God squad, my friendship with Dee was stronger than ever, our team was nationally ranked, and my boyfriend Derek had just started medical school in the Caribbean. This last part helped because having a boyfriend but not actually having to spend time with that boyfriend was the ideal situation for me. Derek and I had been dating for just over two years, after being introduced by one of the girls on the volleyball team when I was a freshman and he was a senior. But once he left for med school, I found myself thinking about our relationship less and less, sometimes not even returning his emails. I also became annoyed when he called, because the connection always had a three-second delay, which only exacerbated the situation. I broke up with him for a couple of months during my sophomore year, eventually requesting we get back together, mostly out of boredom.

One night, while we were driving home from campus after a long day of classes and practice, Dee said to me, "I think this is when the devil will truly test us." She gripped the steering wheel and stared intently at the highway, as if this test could begin at any moment. I asked her to explain what she meant. "The devil knows when you're about to give your life to Christ, and that's when he sets his worst trap for you," she said, glancing at me quickly, then turning back to the road before finishing. "It's like his last-ditch attempt to steal your soul."

Today, those words sound to me like bad copy on the back of a cheesy horror book. But at the time, a shiver passed through me.

I had been reading about hell for so many months that I was beginning to think it might actually exist. At the very least, I desperately wanted to avoid finding out if it did. I also had zero confidence that my faith was strong enough to help me clear whatever hurdle the devil intended to set in my path.

"How do you know this?" I asked Dee.

"I had a long conversation with Lisa after church on Sunday," she answered. "I guess it's a phenomenon of sorts. She told me how the devil tested her last year, and she wanted to warn me about what lies ahead."

"How did the devil test her?"

"She didn't go into specifics," Dee said, as if such details were trivial. "We just need to be vigilant and help each other, spiritually, through whatever may come. Okay?"

"Okay," I said, then spent the rest of the ride staring out my window.

Our weekly FCA gathering was the next night at Dal Ward. Around 7 p.m., those of us attending the fellowship began heading toward the elevators, while my other teammates walked across the hallway to a study room or returned to their dorms and apartments. Normally, not much was required of me at FCA. I would slide into one of the movie theater seats, always next to Dee, and listen to the worship music, which was followed by that night's testimony, often from a former football player who had come back to share how God was shaping his life. But on this particular evening, one of the FCA student leaders bounded onto the stage after the music (*Jesus, Lover Of My Soul!*) and said we were going to break into team-specific groups for a more intimate lesson. The volleyball players moved to one corner of the room, the football players to another, and our basketball team gathered in the front row, just below the stage.

"Let's all take this opportunity to talk through anything heavy on our hearts," we were instructed, the idea being that at the end of the session we would unite in prayer, lifting the burden up to God, who would free us of the emotional weight and help make us a healthier team, spiritually speaking. Of course, before that could happen, we needed to pinpoint the thing that was making our hearts heavy. I looked at my teammates. There were five of us that night, and we were all dressed from head to toe in team-issued Nike apparel. Each year, throughout the season, our director of basketball operations, Kris, released our gear as we needed it. In late August, we were given a Colorado sweatsuit and running sneakers; at the end of October, we got our practice jerseys and shorts, along with basketball shoes; before our first road game, usually in early December, she gave us our travel outfits, which were all-black wind suits, the crinkly kind. And so it went, a steady flow of goodies that prompted us to give Kris the nickname Nike Claus.

Sasha, wearing her black Buffaloes sweatshirt, spoke first in our FCA group. "I've been thinking about Coach Barry a lot lately," she said. Lisa and Kelly began nodding their heads, as if they had been waiting for Sasha to share this exact sentiment. The three of them lived in an off-campus apartment and prayed together every night before bed. "I just think it's important we reach out to her, show her how much we love her," Sasha continued. "Because everybody needs Jesus." She stressed the word *everybody*.

My teammates seemed to understand what Sasha was saying. I did not. I knew that Coach Barry was a "good Catholic girl from Kentucky" (her words) because we had talked about our shared religion during the recruiting process. But unlike me, Coach actually attended church. The previous week, while we were all eating together in Dal Ward, I had overhead Sasha and Kelly asking Coach Barry about her beliefs, and Coach had told them, "Don't worry about me. I know what I believe." So what was this about?

"But Coach is Catholic," I said to the group. "She already has her beliefs." My friends gave me a pitying look, like they were about to break some really bad news. They leaned into the space between us, and Lisa whispered, "Coach Barry's lifestyle is keeping her from truly knowing Jesus."

I glanced at Dee. She was looking down at her hands. I thought I knew what Lisa meant by "lifestyle." During my recruiting visit three years earlier, while most of the team was eating pizza at an Old Chicago, one of the older players had told us that Coach Barry was dating a woman, a professor on campus. The player lowered her voice and looked around the restaurant as she explained that Coach Barry kept her private life hush-hush, because that kind of information could hurt recruiting. "Of course, I probably shouldn't tell you that," she said with a laugh. "Maybe now you won't want to come here." I want to believe my reaction at the time was mild surprise—maybe something like, "Coach dates a woman?"—because I didn't know any real, live lesbians back then. But it's quite possible I might have said, "That is so gross!" The sad truth is that I occasionally uttered homophobic statements in an attempt to convince my audience, and especially myself, that I was heterosexual, despite a growing pile of emotional evidence to the contrary.

I leaned into our circle and whispered, "Wait, so we think Coach Barry is going to . . ." I stopped short of saying "hell" because I didn't like floating that idea out into the universe, in case the spiritual powers that be should somehow misinterpret my words and mistakenly seal her fate. "I mean, we don't think she'll be saved?"

Lisa slowly, solemnly shook her head, never breaking eye contact with me. "It's not our job as Christians to judge, so we have to keep that in mind," she said. "But the life she has chosen is ungodly."

"We can never know someone else's relationship with Christ," Sasha said, picking up the thread from Lisa. "But we do know that certain sins create a gulf between people and God. And this is one of those sins."

My teammates continued to explain their concerns, which they said came from a place of love and acceptance, because Coach Barry

was an important person in their lives and they wanted her to walk
a "healthier" path. I listened as each of them took turns speaking,
occasionally interrupting one another with reminders that none of
this was about passing judgment, which prompted another round
of head nodding. "Absolutely—of course not," someone would say.
"That's not what this is about." Dee didn't speak, but she nodded at
the right times. I stuffed my hands in the pouch of my hooded
sweatshirt and didn't contradict a word that was said.

"Let's pray," Sasha said finally, bowing her head and reaching
for the hands on either side of her. We all linked palms and dropped
our eyes. I stared at the tops of my sneakers, wanting to process all
of this information with my thoughts grounded in reality, rather than
closing my eyes and letting my mind float to some ethereal place,
where only the earnest words of my zealous teammates would fill
the space. Sasha inhaled deeply before speaking. "Heavenly Father,
we love you so much," she said, the words like a passionate exhale.
"We're just so thankful for nights like tonight, when we can open up
our hearts and minds to you, Lord. We know that you made us in your
likeness, just as you made Jesus, and we want to loyally serve you,
God, which is why we come to you tonight with heavy hearts."

Here, Sasha paused and drew another deep breath, preparing
for the verbal challenge ahead. "God, we lift Coach Barry up to you
tonight. We ask that you put your healing hand on her shoulder and
steer her away from her sinful lifestyle. We humbly ask this of you,
Heavenly Father, because we know of your power and goodness. We
are awed by it." She continued for another minute, saying the same
thing in three or four different ways, before ending with, "And thank
you so much for your son."

Sasha must have squeezed her right hand, which was holding
Lisa's left, because Lisa now began speaking, working through the
same prayer while using slightly different words. I continued staring
at my sneakers, eyes wide open, and tapped my right heel, counting
each time the rubber sole met the thin carpet. I reached fifty taps

as Lisa was finishing. I felt her squeeze my left palm twice, quickly, signaling that it was my turn. I allowed the pulse to pass through my body like a wave, flowing across my shoulders and down my arm into my right hand. Then I squeezed Dee's palm without saying a word. She seemed caught off guard, as if I had whipped her a pass she wasn't expecting.

"I . . . um . . ." Dee stammered. Her palm was sweaty in mine, and she removed it, dried it quickly against her thigh, then slid back into my grasp and found her voice. "God," she said, "I just thank you so much for putting these wonderful women in my life as mentors, for showing me the path you want for us . . ."

As Dee and I walked to her car after FCA, we said nothing. I gripped the straps of my backpack as if someone might try to pry it from my shoulders. Dee slipped behind the wheel and I climbed into the passenger's seat, holding my bag tightly against my lap. I had so many questions to ask her: *Do you feel the same way they feel? Is Coach Barry really going to hell?* But I said nothing. She turned on her CD player, filling the car with the vocal gyrations of Elvis singing "Hound Dog."

—⁓—

I was in eighth grade when it happened, the first time I had feelings for a girl. Of course, I didn't know back then what those feelings meant. I just thought everyone got nervous and tingly around cool new people they desperately hoped to be friends with and may or may not have wanted to kiss. Meanwhile, I had also grown out my hair, which gave me a hint of self-confidence. I'd kept it short for years after The Haircut, mostly because the process of growing it out seemed both torturous and a public admission that I was embarrassed about the way I looked. I imagined all of the kids snickering behind my back, saying things like, "What took her so long? She's so weird." But the summer before eighth grade, I let my hair get shaggy, and by that fall, it was just long enough for a small ponytail. Strands of it would continually escape from the elastic band, but I tucked them behind my ears. I didn't care that I had to keep fussing with it; all that mattered was that I could pull some of it through the band, which immediately signaled my gender to everyone around me. I could now confidently walk into any public women's bathroom.

That same fall, I started attending open gym sessions at the high school, which is where I met Nicole, a sophomore on the varsity basketball team. My dad had encouraged me to go, saying it would be good preparation for tryouts and that I needed to show the coaches I was serious about making the team. I knew he was right, so I swallowed my nerves and arrived early for the first session. I was hoping to get there before anyone else, but one girl was already in the gym. I slinked along the sideline and stayed close to the bleachers, which were pushed back against the wall, making the main court look bigger and more imposing than it usually did. I found a spot sufficiently away from where the other girl had put her stuff, then sat on the floor, placing my basketball sneakers next to me. I lifted my eyes and watched as the girl—she had a long, shiny, black ponytail—launched a shot from behind the three-point line. Her release looked like a catapult slinging backward, but the ball arced through the air and dropped through the net. She jogged after it, her ponytail bouncing behind her. I noticed she was wearing low-cut socks, so low you couldn't see them at all above her high tops. I looked down at my own socks, which reached about midway up my shin. My heart started beating faster. My socks were uncool, pathetic even.

"Hey," a voice called. I raised my eyes. The girl with the ponytail was looking at me, pinning the ball against her hip.

"Hi," I said, feeling small.

"Hurry up and come shoot with me."

"Okay," I answered, lifting my sneakers off the floor to show her that I was about to lace them. She shrugged, turned away and took another shot, making that one, too. I looked down at my socks, panicky. I'd finally lost weight and grown out my hair, and yet I still somehow managed to be a dork. I pulled the socks up as far as they would go, a few inches below my knees, then folded them down on themselves. The double layer reached all the way to my toes, but at least now the tops of the socks were much lower, barely above my ankles. I pulled on my sneakers and realized instantly that wearing my socks like this was going to be uncomfortable. I could tell they wanted to slip off my heels, and the bunching by my toes was annoying. I didn't care. I stuffed the rest of the visible material down into my sneakers, further increasing the discomfort. I stood and looked down at my feet, pleased. As I walked onto the court, I felt like I had jammed a facecloth into each shoe. I was also fairly sure that my socks could quit on me at any second.

I jogged underneath the rim and waited for the next shot. The gym was worn down—they were building a new one at the back of the school that would be open by the time I reached ninth grade—but I still felt out of place on such a huge court. What was I, an uncool eighth grader, doing inside the high school gym? I took a deep breath and tried to quell my anxiety. My hands were shaking as I watched the ball fly through the air and clank off the back of the rim. I ran after the rebound, then tossed the ball back to the girl, who caught it with a look of surprise and sent it right back to me. "I missed," she said. "So now it's your turn."

I let the ball roll into my hands, feeling the leather, then dribbled a few times, each bounce pumping me with confidence. I was good at this game, I reminded myself. I could shoot. I could dribble. I knew what I was doing. I dribbled a few more times, standing beyond the three-point line, then put the ball behind my back and drove to the basket for a layup, ever mindful of my father's advice. (*The best shooters never start from the three-point line; they gradually ease into the motion.*) I caught the ball as it dropped through the net and quickly whipped a bounce pass out to my new gym mate.

"I'm Nicole," she said. "What's your name?"

"Kate."

"Ohhhhhhh," she answered, launching an off-balance shot, not seeming to care whether she made it or missed. "You're the little phenom we've all been hearing so much about."

My heart leapt into my throat as the ball slammed off the backboard. I was grateful for the distraction of chasing down another long rebound. But this time I kept the ball, looking over at Nicole. She seemed pleased with herself, a sly grin appearing at the corner of her mouth. She had large brown eyes beneath perfectly kept eyebrows, and a strand of hair had escaped her ponytail and was framing her face. I thought about how to respond, knowing most of my options would sound conceited. "Oh, I don't know about that," I said, then dribbled in for another lay-up. As I landed, one of my socks slid off my heel and bunched around my arch.

When the final pick-up game ended a couple of hours later, I walked over to my stuff and sat down with my back against the bleachers. Gratefully, I removed my sneakers and fixed my socks. I had survived the evening, playing well and presenting myself as at least somewhat cool. Nicole walked over to me. She was already in her sweats and running sneakers, ready to leave the gym. She leaned down and offered me a high five. "Nice games," she said, and winked at me. Then she turned to go, her ponytail whipping against the back of her sweatshirt.

I gulped. A hundred thoughts flew through my mind, like a flock of birds appearing out of nowhere: *Can we be friends? When can I see her again? Does she like me? How can I make her like me? I hope she likes me. What the hell is happening? Why do I care so much? What is wrong with me?*

I told myself it was nothing.

That flock would show up again and again over the years, often when I least expected it. One such moment came the following summer, after my freshman year of high school, during an AAU tournament in Albany. My teammates and I were cooling down between games, sitting cross-legged on the court in our oversized shorts and t-shirts, sipping Gatorade as we watched the action around us. A girl from another local team walked past our group, and when she was out of ear shot, one of my teammates leaned into our little huddle and said, "I heard she's a lesbian." We all recoiled, as if someone had thrown a dead rat into the space between us.

"That's so disgusting," said one of my friends, shaking her head, trying to fling the thought from her mind.

"Yeah," said another, "totally sickening."

"Totally," I chimed in, the flock of birds tearing through my insides.

CHAPTER 6

Eating Pizza and Converting Souls

I was sitting in the athlete computer lab when Sasha walked in, spotted me in the corner, and sat in front of the machine to my right. The small, rectangular-shaped room held about a dozen work stations and was located around the corner from the cafeteria in Dal Ward. This was where we typed our papers and sent emails and wasted time during hours of mandatory study hall. I watched Sasha out of the corner of my eye. She sat still, seemingly waiting for me, so I turned to her.

"You ready?" she asked, standing from her cushioned swivel chair. It was the middle of my junior season, and Sasha was now taking graduate courses while working as a strength and conditioning coach in Dal Ward, figuring out her next step in life. (Her college career had ended the previous spring, when we lost to Oklahoma in the Elite Eight of the NCAA tournament.)

"Ready for . . ." I began to say, then remembered I was supposed to have dinner that night with Sasha and some girl named Cass, a member of the track team who was openly atheist and enjoyed debating the merits and relevance of religion. "Oh yeah," I interrupted myself. "Dinner with the atheist. Give me five minutes."

"Pick you up out front," Sasha said, disappearing from the room.

I still didn't understand why Sasha had invited me to this dinner. I assumed she had asked some other friends first, but they couldn't make it. And since Dee was busy finishing an important mid-semester art project, I guess that left Sasha with only one option as a zealous sidekick. Me! When Sasha and I spent time together, it was often better if we didn't actually speak, because we tended to get our signals crossed. I would say something I thought clearly sounded like a joke, and she'd respond, "Wow, really?" Then I'd have to explain, "No, not really. I'm kidding." Sometimes she tried to get in on the game and attempt a joke of her own, but it usually zoomed over my head because I didn't think she had a particularly good sense of humor. So it was safer for us just to turn on the radio, which is what we did that night while driving to dinner. (Whenever I hear Gloria Estefan's "Rhythm Is Gonna Get You," I think of Sasha, who once said while that song was playing, "Gosh, I sure hope so," making light of her extraordinarily bad dancing skills. She said this earnestly, solemnly shaking her head, and was surprised when everyone in the car began laughing.)

We arrived at BJ's Restaurant and Brewhouse before Cass, so Sasha slid into a booth across from the bar. She motioned for me to sit next to her, on the same side. I thought this odd, but settled in beside her anyway, facing the restaurant's entrance. As we waited for Cass, I thought how silly we looked, like an overeager welcoming committee. I pictured us smiling and waving—such happy robots!— when Cass appeared at the entrance. In the meantime, Sasha rummaged through her backpack and pulled out her worn leather Bible. She put it on the table between us. I looked down at the brown cover and felt a pang of embarrassment, as if we had placed a sign on our table that read, "Go Away."

When people passed by, some spotted the Bible, then looked at us to see who exactly had placed the holy book on a brewhouse table. But Boulder is an eclectic place, possessing the kind of natural hypocrisy that comes when hippies mature into adults with big bank accounts. In Boulder, an environmentalist can drive a Hummer without a drip of irony. It's also a liberal-leaning college town in a traditionally red state; about ninety minutes down the highway, in Colorado Springs, is the home base for Focus on the Family, the right-wing, anti-gay organization determined to preserve the American Way of Life. Which is to say, Boulder has its share of traditional Christians, so I'm sure some people who walked by our table didn't find it strange to see a Bible resting next to the silverware.

Cass arrived a few minutes later. She looked rushed. I would come to learn that she had more friends than she could really keep content. She liked it this way, always having a call to answer, a dinner to attend, somewhere else to be. When she walked toward our booth, I recognized her from the Dal Ward weight room, so I smiled. Cass smiled, too, then slid onto the leather seat across from us. She had golden brown hair, curly, and was wearing it down; it fell to just above her shoulders. Her features appeared perfectly crafted, and her skin seemed slightly bronzed, as if she had returned from a beach vacation the week before. Brown freckles, matching her eyes, were sprinkled across the top of her cheeks, like they had dripped off her eyelashes.

Once she settled into her seat, Cass folded her arms on the table, leaned forward, and looked at us expectantly, as if to say, "So whatcha got for me?" Sasha placed her hand on the Bible and seemed about to say something when the waiter interrupted, handing each of us a menu. This broke the spell, and Cass leaned back in her seat, pondering the dinner options.

"What's the track team like?" I asked, because I was fascinated with how other teams operated at Colorado and because I didn't want the first thing I said to this woman to be a quote from the Bible. Cass looked up from the menu and met my gaze. She said something about the track team, about practice times I think, but I couldn't concentrate on her words because suddenly my heart started beating faster. I had been starving when Sasha and I walked into the restaurant; now when I glanced at the menu, I felt a pang of nausea, and none of the food seemed appealing. I leaned forward, toward the tinted yellow plastic cup in front of me, and put the straw to my lips, taking a deep pull of ice water. I looked again at Cass, who was looking at me. A small smile crossed her lips. I looked away first.

Once we ordered, Sasha brought up the topic we were ostensibly there to discuss: converting Cass to Christianity. Cass appeared mildly amused as Sasha launched into her speech about the splendors of Christ, about his infinite capacity for both love and forgiveness, about how he loves all of us equally, despite our many sins. What Sasha didn't understand was that Cass already had her beliefs. She believed in the beauty of the world around us. She believed that climbing a mountain on a Sunday morning brought joy to your soul, and that taking a walk among the trees and birds connected you to the earth, which seemed to her a better thing to worship than the man presented in the stories of the book resting next to Sasha's silverware.

"How can you believe in a God who sends people to hell?" Cass asked.

"God gives each of us free will," Sasha said. "We make our own decisions. It pains him when we turn our backs on him. He wants desperately for each of us to find the light."

Cass tilted her head and paused, as if giving Sasha a chance to recognize that she hadn't actually answered the question. After a few awkward seconds, Cass raised her eyebrows and said, "I also don't understand a God who says that it's wrong, evil, for me to love another woman."

Sasha began talking. I looked at Cass, who glanced quickly at me, then turned her attention back to Sasha as if nothing interesting had just happened. As if she had not just said, in so many easy, carefree words, that she loved women. As if this beautiful, intelligent, charming woman—proudly, openly gay—had not just turned the conversation upside-down and spun my world off its axis. I wrapped my right hand around the plastic cup of water, clutching it the way I would grab a door handle in a car that was flying around a tight turn.

I realized I was holding my breath, so I let the air out slowly and lifted my eyes to watch Cass. Her lips were slightly parted, her eyes clear as she listened to Sasha, who was gesticulating about the wonders and pitfalls of the free will that God had given to each of us. ("He could have created humans to worship him, but he wants us to *choose* to love him.") The idea of free will always seemed like the ace in the hole for Christians. Why do bad things happen? Because God has completely relinquished control over our actions. Any human behavior that makes you question the existence of God is the sole fault of humanity, while all of our beautiful moments are a pure reflection of him. The lack of consistency, and the logic flaws, had already started poking holes in my flimsy belief structure.

As I watched Cass listen, I could see she was inspecting each of Sasha's arguments, finding them wanting, and tossing them out. "The God of the Bible," Cass said, gently touching the corner of Sasha's book, "says that love is the most important part of being human." At this, Sasha nodded. "So then," Cass continued, "would that same God have me go through life without knowing true love?" I tried to find a gap in Cass' argument but could not. Her words hung in the air for a second, and I expected Sasha to offer a Christian response, but instead Sasha turned to me. She was resting her chin on her closed fist. Cass turned to me, too.

"Free will," I said, and looked at Cass, trying to put a twinkle in my eyes. "I think it's about free will." I could see Cass swallow a smile. Sasha kept watching me for a few seconds to see if I was going to further explain my answer. I did not.

Sasha jumped back in. "What Kate is trying to say is that everyone has a cross to bear, so to speak. Each of us must sacrifice things in order to follow Jesus. No one ever said being a Christian was the easiest road. There are temptations everywhere: alcohol,

drugs, sex, people who want to lead us into sin. God asks that we turn away from the things that will separate us from him. And in turn he will give us a kind of love we could never imagine."

She pulled her Bible toward her and began flipping through the pages. I borrowed the pen that had been resting next to the spine of the book—Sasha always kept one near in case a verse struck her as worthy of underlining—and grabbed a cocktail napkin from the stack the waiter had left on our table. The restaurant's colorful logo was stamped onto the center of the white square, so I scribbled in the top left corner. The blue ink blotted in the middle of the T, my first letter, as I wrote, "This could be a long night!" I capped the pen and slid the napkin across the table, careful to avoid the spots where condensation from our drinks had puddled. Cass read my words, keeping her eyes down. I had not allowed myself to think about why I was writing the note or what she might think of it. I just knew I wanted to open a different line of communication with her, one that wasn't shared by Sasha or dedicated to religion. Without raising her eyes, Cass motioned for the pen. I rolled it across to her. She scribbled in a different corner and sent the napkin back across the polished wood table.

I let my hand rest on the corner of the note as Sasha popped her head out of the Bible. "Here it is," she said, pressing her finger to the verse she wanted to share. I could feel the tiny ridges of the napkin beneath my finger, and I swirled the square around so Cass' words were facing in the right direction. As Sasha began reading, I looked down and saw what Cass had written.

"I hope . . ."

My favorite part was the ellipsis, eagerly racing into the future with no end in sight.

—⁂—

"What do you think?" Sasha asked as she put the key into the ignition of her Rav4. We were parked in the covered garage behind Pearl

Street, and I laughed at her question, because trying to articulate what I was thinking would probably have required hours of therapy, not a quick car ride home. She looked at me strangely, then backed out of the spot.

"Cass seems like she knows what she believes," I eventually answered, and Sasha seemed relieved I had said something.

"The devil really has a hold of her," she said. She was tapping the steering wheel, trying, but failing, to keep the rhythm of the song on the radio. She seemed unaware of the gravity of her statement, because when I glanced at her to see if she was completely serious, she frowned and gave me a sad little nod, like, *Yup . . . oh well.*

That's when I tuned out. I felt transparent, as if everything I was feeling could be seen on my face, so I turned away from Sasha and looked out the window, saying nothing for the rest of the car ride. She dropped me off in the dirt parking lot at the base of the hill behind Dal Ward. "See you tomorrow," she said, as I stepped out of her car and into my own. I watched her little green SUV bop out of the lot, catching every pothole along the way, her headlights illuminating the trees along the creek. I wrapped my hands around the steering wheel of my Honda Accord, a hand-me-down from my mother, and squeezed the plastic as tightly as I could. Then I rested my forehead on the wheel and closed my eyes.

The way I felt in that moment—tingly, no appetite, my mind constantly drifting toward Cass—was hardly new for me. I had felt it many times before. The previous year, I had found myself looking forward to 6 a.m. lifting sessions, popping out of bed at 5:30 in the morning, because I would get to see my new teammate Ashley, who had transferred from the University of Florida. At night, I would log onto AOL Instant Messenger and look for Ashley's screen name, concocting some reason to send her a note. She was seeing some guy at Colorado State, and I was dating Derek. I told myself she was just a cool new friend—what's the big deal?

But Cass had just exposed the lie, the one I wasn't even fully aware I'd been telling myself. It was like she had shined a flashlight into some secret compartment inside my heart, and I think I knew that everything packed away in there was about to demand examination.

CHAPTER 7

Who Here Struggles with Homosexuality?

"What's going on with you?" Dee asked, as we walked toward the home of Chrissy, the FCA leader and host of that week's Bible study. Chrissy's house was a suburban wonder, deftly constructed to look different than the houses on either side, when actually just the kitchen and the garage had switched places on the blueprint. A long cement walkway intersected the front lawn, and the bright sun was reflecting off it. I held my Bible in my right hand, squinting.

"What do you mean?" I said, even though I knew exactly what Dee meant and why she was asking. For the past forty-eight hours, ever since meeting Cass, I had lived mostly inside my own head. I had heard very little of what Dee said to me, and I think she finally became intrigued about why I had checked out of our usually interesting conversations.

"You . . . you're totally vacant," she said, then paused. "No, that's not right. You're the opposite of vacant. You seem consumed. So what is it?"

I could talk to Dee. I could tell her anything. I knew that. And I wanted to talk to her, right then and there. I wanted to stop in the middle of that blinding walkway and unload everything, letting the words and emotions spill between us. I believed she would help me carry all of it. If I asked her, she would get back in the car with me and drive away; she would skip the Bible study so we could talk. I opened my mouth and breathed deeply. Then I shook my head.

"I'm not sure yet," I said. "But when I am, I'll tell you."

She considered my words and smiled.

We walked into the oversized front hallway of the house. There were rooms sprouting in each direction, an endless sea of off-white carpeting. The girls were in the back room, "the TV room," which featured a floral couch, frilly curtains, and one square black TV in the corner, on top of an oak chest. I took off my sneakers and shuffled through the house. Dee trailed me, her size-13 feet like paddles.

"Ladies!" Chrissy raised her arms in celebration when she saw us and rose from the carpet, where she had been sitting. At Bible studies, many of us chose the hardness of the floor over the couch, as a show of humility in honor of Jesus. Those who ended up on the couch, when the circle of people on the floor was too crowded, almost had an air of frustration, as if sitting on the floor scored more points with Jesus. It was the Christian equivalent of holding the door for a woman with a baby stroller—a simple act, at little inconvenience, with a Good Samaritan payoff.

Chrissy wrapped me in a long hug, rocking me back and forth; then she did the same with Dee. "We're so glad you're both here," she said. "I was just about to start today's lesson."

I sat down on the corner of the couch and hugged a pillow tightly to my chest. Dee sat on the other end, with two people between us. My Bible rested on the arm of the couch, precariously balanced. I placed my palm on the leather cover and steadied the book. I was attending the Bible study out of habit and desperation. Could Jesus actually give me answers? I wanted to believe what my teammates had told me, that he could calm my heart and provide peace. Because at that moment, the pull of what Cass had introduced into my life possessed the energy of a tornado, whereas Jesus was like a little face fan blowing in the corner, barely disturbing a strand of hair—and about to get swept away in the oncoming storm.

I had prayed just the night before. *Take this away, God, please. Make my heart still and calm again, and I will follow you. I promise I will try harder.* I uttered these words in the middle of the night, wide awake in my corner bedroom, the lamp on my nightstand providing a circle of soft yellow light, like a halo, in the darkness. I was kneeling, my elbows resting on the mattress, my forehead pinned to my clasped hands— the very picture of desperation. I even stopped praying for a second to recognize what a cliché I had become. I took a snapshot in my mind, told myself to never forget the kind of emptiness I felt and the weakness I was displaying. I asked Jesus for help, over and over. And then I waited.

Jesus didn't show. An hour later, with my heart still feeling unhinged and my hands trembling, I pulled myself onto the bed and chastised myself. What the fuck was I even thinking? I was pathetic, hopeless, and maybe even gay. But how was that possible? I couldn't be gay. No way. No. I just couldn't. That would explode like a bomb in my life, sending everyone—friends, teammates, coaches, family— scattering.

"So . . ." Chrissy began, opening her Bible. "Let's turn to Romans."

I pulled my Bible onto the pillow on my lap and quickly breezed through it, like it was one of those picture books that make a movie when you flick through the pages fast enough. I fixated on the upper right corner to see if I could spot the word "Romans" flying past. Fuuuuuck! Was Romans in the Old Testament or the New? Seems like Romans would be in the Old, because wasn't Rome important a really long time ago? But then again, everything in the Bible was a long time ago. It's not like the New Testament has a "SoCal" chapter. Without moving my head, I darted my eyes to the right, to the girl sitting next to me, to get a roundabout idea of where Romans was located. She was a little more than midway through the book and was carefully turning pages one by one, the final slowdown before pulling into her Bible parking spot. I recognized her as a volleyball player. She knew exactly where to find Romans.

"Turn to Romans 1:26," Chrissy continued. She was looking around, waiting for each of us to look up, which signaled we had read the verse and were ready to absorb some wisdom that would complement God's words. I finally found Romans and lifted my head, without having read the verse, because it felt like everyone was waiting for me. Chrissy nodded, so I nodded back, little puppet that I was. I'm ready! Once she started speaking again, I looked back down to check out Romans 1:26.

"This lesson has been weighing on my heart for many weeks," Chrissy said. "I want each of you to come at this verse with an open heart and mind, and to know that we are in a safe space, surrounded by God's love."

I pinned my finger to the tiny number 26 that existed like a footnote on the extra-thin paper. I began reading silently: "Because of this, God gave them over to shameful lusts. Even their women exchanged natural sexual relations for unnatural ones." My eyes darted to Dee, to see what she was doing. Her head was tilted down, her eyes on her own Bible; I could see them moving from left to right, then back again. She seemed to be reading the verses surrounding The Verse, looking for additional context. I looked at Chrissy, who was also engrossed in her Bible.

"Let's read God's word together," Chrissy said a moment later. "Romans 1:26 says, 'Because of this, God gave them over to shameful lusts. Even their women exchanged natural sexual relations for unnatural ones.'"

Chrissy closed her Bible, but her hand was still bookmarking the page. She looked around the room and asked, "Who here struggles with homosexuality?"

—⚟—

The only other time in my life I had felt so exposed was in sixth grade, the last year I kept my hair short after the Hot Cuts experiment. I had thought my mom's sadness was a one-time response to that initial chop-off, not an ongoing emotion she would feel each time she looked at me—her baby daughter, the tomboy. I believed I had struck an irreversible blow, destroying her image of me as the cute, curly headed daughter. So I didn't grow out my hair right away because I didn't think it would fix anything.

As a result of the emotional price tag, I never truly loved that haircut, even though it was exactly what I wanted. There were a few months, maybe almost a year, when it seemed like a non-issue. I was eight years old, about to turn nine, and still young enough to be out of the reach of society's brutal gender assessments and the cruelty that kids wield like rocks as they get older. The boys weren't yet interested in girls; the girls weren't yet obsessed with which of them had the boys' attention. We were a relatively indistinguishable mass of youthful energy, and I just happened to have short hair.

Of course, at some point all of this changed. And while it certainly didn't happen like a lightning strike, charring the ground in an instant, that's how it felt to me. I was sitting in my science classroom, perched on a stainless steel stool, my bag in front of me on the chunky wooden table. Class was scheduled to begin, but our teacher was absent and the room was filling with the kind of exuberance that brews when kids are left unattended. Right before the excitement turned into chaos, the door flew open. An adult pushed through, out of breath, as if he had jogged through the long hallway. His presence quickly quieted the class, until we recognized him as the substitute teacher—a toy for us to play with!—and a different kind of energy enveloped the room. The man fumbled in his bag, eventually pulling out the class roster. He stood in front of the blackboard and looked down at the manila folder in his hands; then he looked out at us. He did this a few times before he called out the first name: Leslie Adams. She was sitting in the first row, and slowly raised her hand in a totally bored kind of way. When the teacher nodded, she rolled her eyes and began inspecting her fingernails. The substitute made a mark in his folder. Then he continued calling out names alphabetically and scribbling notes.

"Kate Fagan," he said eventually, keeping his head down for an extra second. "Here," I answered, raising my hand. Until this moment, I enjoyed having substitute teachers, because the class was usually such a waste of time that I could read my book or just tune out. Basically, the substitute's only job was to make sure we didn't kill each other. Plus, until this moment, I was one of the cooler kids in sixth grade. The boys loved me because I was on the baseball team, and the girls found me interesting because the boys did. I was living the short-hair dream.

"Kate Fagan," the teacher said again, his eyes up now. I raised my hand an inch higher, assuming he hadn't seen me the first time. My classmates turned to look at me, then back at the teacher. Their eyes bounced between us like they were watching a tennis match. Finally, the sub locked eyes with me and nodded. He marked his sheet, then tossed out the following sentence, absentmindedly, as if simply thinking out loud.

"Oh, okay," he said. "I was just expecting a girl."

His words appeared in my mind like puzzle pieces. Did he not think I was a girl? Had he just called me a boy? I quickly arranged the words in the proper order. The result was like a stun gun to the heart, and I melted into my seat. I hoped that my classmates hadn't heard. Or that maybe they would be confused by his sentence, too. I looked straight ahead at the chalkboard and didn't move a muscle, wishing my stillness would somehow make me invisible. The air rushed away from me as my classmates sucked in their breath—the deep kind you take just before exploding into laughter. I kept my eyes forward. How had I suddenly arrived in this place? It felt like a trick, like the sun had been shining one second, and now snow was falling. My eyes burned.

I wanted to cry. I wanted to grab my bag and run for the door. I wanted to sprint down the hallway and out of the building. I wanted to run the mile back to my house, curl up in a ball on my bed, and cry myself to sleep. Instead, as I sat there staring at the green chalkboard, nothing felt more important than acting cool and collected, like the whole thing was no big deal to me. My eyes filled with tears. My vision became blurry. But I didn't blink. I told myself crying would make everything worse.

The teacher lifted his eyes from the folder and glanced around the room. He tilted his head and looked at me, then slowly lowered the folder, and I could see now that he was wearing a Ralph Lauren sweater. I stared for a second at the logo, at the man playing polo on the upper left corner. I shrugged at the sub, and for some reason I felt like I owed him an apology, as if this disruption had been my fault. Because I was the one who had put him in a bad spot, right? What was he supposed to think when he looked at me, with my short hair and my baseball jersey? I swallowed the tears and pretended to chuckle, while turning my palms upward, in an "Oops!" gesture. I couldn't escape the nauseating blend of emotions—fear, embarrassment, sadness—but I could throw a blanket over them by playing along, like I'd been in on the joke the whole time. Then I waited for the laughter to die, which it did, gradually, like a heavy metal song bleeding to nothing.

It wasn't until that day in science class that I truly understood why my mother had cried when I cut my hair. She had an image in her mind of what I should look like, who I should be, and a lot of that had to do with the belief that my life would be easier to navigate if I conformed to society's standards. Girls have long hair and date boys. Anyone else is asking for trouble.

—⚉—

The words hung in the air, like a basketball that would decide the outcome of a game, in that moment where it's still going up, just before it starts coming down.

Who here struggles with homosexuality?

That Sunday in the back room of Chrissy's house, I kept my eyes on my Bible, pretending to be busy absorbing a side dish of Romans—I just can't get enough of this stuff!—while we all waited to see what would happen next. Chrissy, a former college volleyball player, was tall and stocky, with long blonde hair. She was married to a guy who had played football at Colorado and, briefly, in the NFL. I think many of my teammates thought she was living the Christian dream: a God-fearing husband who led the couple in nightly prayer, an oversized house in the suburbs, a job with FCA that she seemed passionate about. But I always sensed a hint of sadness in her that she seemed to paint over with a too-bright smile.

Chrissy seemed to think the day's lesson would turn into a conversation, that one or two of us would confess to homosexual thoughts, and the rest of the group would lay their hands on the sinners and ask Jesus to wipe our minds of unnatural desires. But that didn't happen; none of us said a word. We just sat there in silence for the longest minute ever. There were eight of us at the Bible study, including Chrissy. Four girls sat on the long floral couch, with me on one end and Dee on the other. On the floor in front of us, sitting at the coffee table, were Sasha and two volleyball players, all three of them holding pens suspended over blank sheets of paper, seemingly ready to jot down names if necessary. I pretended to check the clock on the back wall, taking a quick, sweeping look around the group to see if I could detect a tick or a slight grimace on anyone's face, something external that would reveal the internal struggle.

"Then I'll start us off!" Chrissy said finally, and much too cheerily, launching into an awkward speech sprinkled with Bible verses. "It's not unusual for women playing team sports to struggle with feelings of homosexuality. We all spend so much time around one another, it's easy to confuse feelings of respect and admiration for carnal desire. But God tells us there are different kinds of love."

I stayed still in my little corner of the couch, because even the slightest movement might draw unwanted attention. *Why was Kate fidgeting during this lesson? Was something making her uncomfortable?* I could picture Sasha turning over her shoulder—she was sitting at my feet—and asking, "Is everything okay?" But at the same time, I knew I needed to behave somewhat naturally, otherwise someone might become suspicious. *Kate seems to be holding her breath. What's got her so tense? Homosexual struggles, perhaps?* I coughed, trying hard to make it one of those coughs that says, "No big deal everybody. I'm totally at ease right now and tuned into the lesson—just coughing because I had to cough."

Chrissy continued: "Who here knows what 'agape love' means?"

I saw Sasha start to raise her hand, then stop, realizing we weren't in a formal classroom. "It's a godly kind of love," she said. "It's not a sexual love, but a pure love, one human being for another—a loving friendship, which God blesses."

"Yes!" Chrissy exclaimed, smiling. "Exactly. And the key part of 'agape' is that God smiles on those relationships. They please God. He takes great pleasure in seeing his children love one another." With a smile still pasted on her lips, Chrissy allowed us all a moment to process the soft, beautiful wonder of a godly friendship. *Agape . . .* the word itself sounded lush and radiant, and I noticed that she seemed to be staring off into the distance, as if watching puppies play.

Suddenly, she frowned. "Homosexuality is the opposite of agape," she said. "And I know this intimately." She closed her Bible and laid it down in front of her, a signal that the upcoming lesson would come from Chrissy's heart, not God's word. "A good friend of mine struggled with homosexuality while we played college volleyball together. It was heartbreaking. We spent many tear-filled nights together as she battled to rid herself of these unwanted feelings. What I learned is that no one chooses to feel this way, but they do choose to either fight the feelings or succumb to them."

She did not say what her friend had chosen.

Chrissy was resting her elbows on her thighs, her hands dangling over the edge of her knees. She dropped her head for a second so we could all process this hard-earned wisdom. I used the free moment to glance again at Dee, who had a far-away look in her eyes. When Chrissy started speaking again, she took us on a tour of the Bible, making pit stops at all of the key anti-gay verses. I made a show of flipping through my Bible, but I abstained from seeking out the specified passages because I had seen them all before, and reading them again in that moment would have been too much self-flagellation. Chrissy kept talking, hammering home each verse with an anecdote or two. Finally, she paused and looked at each of us with deep and soulful eyes, wrapping up the lesson with this final thought: "Ladies, my beloved sisters in Christ, we can find answers to all things if we read God's word with our hearts open to receive his grace. Please know that choosing to live a homosexual lifestyle is a choice against God."

She waited a beat, then shook, as if trying to rid herself of a bad case of the heebie-jeebies. "Now that that's done, let's pray!" Chrissy said enthusiastically, offering her hands to the women nearest her. "Heavenly Father, we come before you humbled by your awesomeness . . ."

I could not leave that house fast enough.

CHAPTER 8

Is This Heaven? No, It's Iowa

My favorite hotel on the Big 12 circuit was the Gateway in Ames, Iowa. Nightly, there were warm cookies in the lobby—chocolate chip, oatmeal raisin, white chocolate macadamia nut—and they even remained chewy long after they had cooled. The hotel also had pet goldfish that it lent to guests. One of my teammates, Carrie, always requested a goldfish, tenderly carrying it up to her room as if she would love it forever. The Gateway had extra-plush pillows and a dream-like mattress. Compared to the beds in the cheap hotels we usually stayed at in these flyover states, the beds at the Gateway made you feel like you were sleeping on a cloud. These perks balanced out the main problem with the hotel: its location. Ames makes the middle of nowhere look happening.

The cookies were more than just cookies; their very existence was a loophole in the system. You see, while we were on the road, Coach Barry closely monitored our diet. She kept tabs as best she could while we were at home, but really there was nothing she could do to stop us from driving through Taco Bell after a game. She couldn't prevent us from packing a three-pound bag of Skittles in our carry-ons, either—which many of us did—but she could at least strictly control our meals. On the road, the schedule was always the same: We wore our black travel outfits and ate dinner in one of the hotel's conference rooms. There was usually chicken (grilled, no seasoning), along with baked potatoes and rolls (but no butter), and some sort of steamed vegetable (minus the olive oil) that tasted like it had been cooked with an iron. There was never, ever dessert. Some hotels had trinket bowls full of red-and-white striped mints throughout the hallways and lobbies, and we convinced ourselves these were a treat. Every once in a while, a hotel's wait staff would inadvertently put out a bowl of individual pads of butter, and the players would stuff handfuls into our pockets before Coach Barry could correct the mistake. When a waiter removed the bowl, we would stare at the butter longingly as it disappeared into a back room, then frown as we looked down at our dry potatoes. No amount of cottage cheese or fat-free sour cream could satisfy our butter cravings.

I understood Coach Barry's focus on nutrition. We needed every advantage possible. She was fond of the old maxim, "Hard work beats talent when talent doesn't work hard." So we worked hard (when we weren't swiping butter). During my freshman season at Colorado, the day before our first game, Coach Barry had taken us through our game-day routine, step by step, hour by hour. When she got to the part about the pregame dinner, she said, "Eat a balanced meal. I don't want to see anybody tossing back three or four dinner rolls." Because of that, I never ate more than two rolls, scared that if I took a third (they were usually no bigger than the size of a closed fist), Coach would somehow find out and consider it a breach of team policy.

So the cookies at the Gateway in Ames were an anomaly—dessert on the road when we never had dessert on the road. Some of us would occasionally raid the hotel vending machines, but prepackaged candy was dull compared to homemade cookies (even those baked by a Gateway employee). When we stayed at this hotel, before games against Iowa State, I usually ate two oatmeal raisin cookies and spent the rest of the night telling myself I didn't need a third.

The week after I met Cass, and only three days after our "Who Here Struggles With Homosexuality" Bible study, I walked past those freshly baked cookies as if they were a bowl of marbles, totally inedible. I had lost nearly a pound a day since that dinner at BJ's. I was behind in all of my courses because I spent most of class scribbling notes to Cass that I knew I would never give her. And I hadn't done anything productive—like make an outside shot, which was my forte—in our past four basketball practices. Nobody seemed to notice this last part yet. I suppose I had built up enough good will that I could blend in for a few days, slink to the back of the longest lines, go a little slower than top speed (which was necessary because I had no energy) without anyone calling me out. Of course, I knew that wouldn't last much longer. The next night, we had a crucial Big 12 game against Iowa State, and I was a starter averaging 11 points per game. Coach Barry and my teammates were counting on me to make some three-pointers, to play smart and hard, and help us win.

Dee still didn't know what was wrong with me. When I saw her before practice, or at night in the apartment, she regarded me curiously, like I was an undomesticated animal unsure of human interaction. I was still going back and forth in my own mind. *Christians are wrong about gays. Christians are right about gays. I don't actually understand God's stance on gays.* And I kept coming back to two specific flaws in the traditional Christian stance on homosexuality:

1. Why didn't Jesus speak about homosexuality during his time on earth? He addressed a lot of human issues and pretty much laid out a step-by-step blueprint for how to be a good human being, and yet he spoke not a word about (or against) homosexuality, which seems curious given the volatile reactions that many Christians exhibit toward the gay community. According to Christians, God is all-knowing, which means that he could see into the future and would have known the ostracism and persecution that many gays would face. And yet Jesus left the situation muddled.

2. Christians say that God is all-knowing, all-powerful, and all-good. No Christian I know would dispute those characteristics. He is

the Alpha and the Omega, the beginning and the end. No Christian would dispute the following, either: God created me knowing each hair on my head, knowing all of my decisions before I made them, knowing my entire life before I lived it. Which means, according to many Christians, God created me knowing I was gay and knowing I would spend eternity in hell (with all that weeping and gnashing of teeth—yikes!) once my time on Earth ended. But if God knows my heart, which all Christians will tell you he does, then God also knows I don't want to spend eternity in hell, and that if I was destined to do so, I would rather not have been born at all. Who would be okay with an eternity of torture in exchange for seventy-five years or so—a blip, really—of roaming around the planet? My question then, the logic flaw in Christianity, is how can God be "all-good" if he creates people destined for hell even though he knows they don't want to go to hell?

I know many Christians would argue it comes down to free will, that God creates each of us and allows us to make our own choices. I get that. But, again, it doesn't answer the question. How can God be all-good when there is something particularly malicious about creating humans he knows will be going to Hell? At the very least, Christians ought to consider changing the "all-knowing, all-powerful, all-good" label to something like, "all-knowing, all-powerful, and sometimes kinda sucky."

—m—

The night before the game against Iowa State, I was wandering aimlessly through the Gateway, walking the hallways lined with empty conference rooms, trudging up the back stairway meant for use only during a fire, walking across a floor of vacant rooms, then back down the stairs again. Curfew, mandated by Coach Barry, was not for another two hours. I was rooming with one of my younger teammates, whose head would probably explode if I tried to talk through these issues with her. I needed Dee. She needed to carry some of this baggage for me because I was crumbling beneath the weight.

I walked into the elevator and pressed the button for Dee's floor. I stuffed my hands into the pockets of my wind pants and watched the numbers light up as the elevator slowly crept higher. When the doors opened, I was facing a mirror, my reflection partially blocked by a vase of fake flowers. I stepped forward and leaned to the right, to see my entire head. I ran my hand along my hair, which was pulled back in a swirly bun. I leaned forward until my nose was an inch away and my breath fogged the glass. I was expecting my eyes to look dulled, troubled, but they looked the same as they always had. The elevator made a dinging sound behind me, and I backed away from the mirror, not wanting anyone to see me pondering myself. An older man nodded hello as he passed, then turned down the hallway. I followed in his wake, eventually coming to Dee's room.

I knocked on the door. Dee was also rooming with a younger teammate, and I had already decided I would send the player to hang out with my deserted roomie, who was probably wondering where I had gone. (Coach Barry's travel protocol required that each player room with each teammate once before we repeated pairings.) The door was propped open on the deadbolt, so I knocked another time, lightly, to announce my arrival as I entered the room. Dee was sitting in the back corner by the window, with her feet crossed at the ankle and resting on an ottoman. Her Bible was open on her lap. "Kater!" she said when she saw me. She slapped the book closed.

Our teammate Camille was lounging on her bed, flipping through the TV channels. All three of us were still wearing our Colorado travel outfits, black Nike wind suits. Camille said hello, then returned her attention to the screen.

"What are the chances I can kick you out of your own room?" I asked her.

Camille looked at Dee, then back at me. "I don't know," she said with a shrug, like she didn't care either way. "Who are you rooming with?"

"Cheryl."

Camille swung her legs off the bed and stood. "I'll go hang with her for a while," she said.

"Thanks," I replied, and watched her shuffle out of the room, shrewdly removing the deadbolt and fully shutting the door behind her.

"Wow," Dee said. "It's like that, huh?"

I joined her in the back of the room, lowering myself into the armchair that faced hers. All we needed was some bourbon and a couple of pipes. I had no idea what I was going to say, or if I was going to say anything at all. Dee watched me for a minute or two, waiting, then she shrugged, opened her Bible, and started reading again. I think she had decided she was done worrying about what was going on in my head.

We sat like this for a while, with Dee occasionally peering over her Bible to see if I was still sitting there, staring off into space. Finally, she lowered the book and said, "Okay, I give up. Talk to me, would you?"

This was the final bit of encouragement I needed, and I immediately said, "I can't stop thinking about Sunday's Bible study."

Dee nodded. "Go on . . ."

Leaning forward, elbows on knees, I said, "I just keep thinking about what Chrissy was saying, about God being against gays. And, I don't know, I guess something in my heart is telling me it feels all wrong. I just can't see how God would abandon an entire group of people like that."

I did not mention my dinner with Sasha and Cass, the way Cass had struck me, or my own personal stake in how God might feel about gays. I was climbing one mountain at a time. First, I needed to know what Dee had thought of Sunday's lesson, if her personal beliefs mirrored what Chrissy had taught, or if she had formulated her own thoughts. We hadn't spoken much on the drive home from that Bible study. One of us had said, "Well, that was interesting," and then we each stared out our windows, watching the brown plains of Colorado pass by.

"And there's so much hate," I continued. "I don't see how anything in the Bible would lead to this kind of hate against gays. I'm just so confused."

Dee had been nodding, but then she slowly started shaking her head, so I really had no clue what she would say. I rambled around a bit more, saying essentially the same thing in a few different ways. When I finally stopped talking, I looked at my best friend in the whole world and waited. A strand of her brown hair was disobeying, lifting from her scalp despite the product she used to smooth it out.

"I'm so glad you said something," she said. "I've been thinking about this same stuff all week." She held up the Bible. "It's like, there are certain verses in here that say one thing, but when I look into my heart, I feel something completely different."

I had to keep myself from jumping up and wrapping her in an epic, Gays-Are-A-Okay hug. Instead, I emphatically said, "Yes, exactly!" And then, "I can't tell you how relieved I am to hear you say that."

By the time Camille returned, peeking her head slowly around the door to make sure her arrival was safe, Dee and I had spent more than an hour bouncing ideas back and forth about our own beliefs regarding how God feels about homosexuality. Our conclusion was that none of us should judge anyone else's relationship with Christ, a truly personal endeavor. Gays could be Christians; Christians could be gays.

"Come on in," Dee said, waving to Camille. "Kater Tot has to beat curfew, too." (That nickname, Kater Tot, was given to me freshman year by Kelly and instantly embraced by everyone, occasionally shortened to "Tot." Later, our strength and conditioning coach would jokingly call me "Tiny Kate" because of my distinct lack of muscle definition, but Kater Tot was the nickname that stuck.)

I wrapped Dee in the hug I had wanted to give her earlier, and told her I loved her. I also hugged Camille on my way out of the room, which she accepted with the enthusiasm of a mannequin. When I got back to my room, I fell onto my heavenly mattress, beneath my dream-like comforter, and slept better than I had in a week.

With Dee in my corner, I knew I would be okay.

CHAPTER 9

Nothing Worth Having Comes Easily

We flew home from Ames on Thursday, after losing to Iowa State in front of a sold-out crowd. I did not play well. The morning of the game, the morning after my late-night chat with Dee, I had awoken with a new set of worries. The clouds rolled in over my comfortable bed in the Gateway Hotel and blocked out the sun before I could even blink away the sleep. Just because Dee said she supported God and gays, in theory, did not mean she would support me becoming a godly gay, in action. And what would she think when she realized I hadn't told her the full truth about my own feelings?

During the game, at one of the timeouts, I was sitting with the other starters, facing Coach Barry, sweat dripping down my temples, trying to focus on whatever it was she was saying. She was kneeling with a clipboard in front of her, making hard-angle lines with her blue marker. They looked like hieroglyphics. I stared at the scoreboard, at the red bulbs lit up in the shapes of numbers, but I could see only each individual light, meaningless on its own. I was living in a distorted reality. Coach Barry tapped me on the knee and said, "You got that, Kate?" And I nodded, noncommittal, a nod and a shake at the same time, kind of like Dee had done the night before. Coach looked around at the other players who weren't checked into the game, found the one she wanted, and pointed her toward the scorer's table. "Leslie, get in for Kate," she said. I stood, surrendering my seat to Leslie, tossed a towel over my shoulder, and wandered behind the bench, mostly relieved to be out of the way.

The weekend after our loss to Iowa State, Dee decided to invite our teammates over for omelets on Saturday morning. The two of us shared a ground-floor apartment in Niwot, a little town just outside Boulder, with our teammate Lindsay. Dee went to the Safeway a few miles from our apartment and bought two dozen eggs. When she came home, brown paper bags in hand, she said to me, "Oh, and Cass is coming, too. You know that girl from the track team?"

I acted like I was trying to place the name. "Right," I said, taking one of the bags from her hands. "I know who you mean." I followed Dee to the small galley kitchen. "So why'd you invite her?" I asked, making sure to keep my voice as level as possible. I didn't want my question to sound like, "Why'd *you* invite her?" Or, even worse, "Why'd you invite *her*?" I made sure to softly hop from one word to the next, as if none of them were all that important.

Dee pulled open the fridge and peered inside, extending an empty hand toward me without looking. I handed her the first dozen eggs. "We started talking in the computer lab yesterday," she said. "She's super cool, so I invited her over. Not sure if she'll come."

"Yeah, she's cool, right?" I answered, handing Dee the bag of shredded cheese.

"Yeah, and . . ." Dee peeked her head out and raised her eyebrows, in a *get this* kind of way. "She's an atheist."

"Wow," was all I could manage, while passing Dee the second carton of eggs.

"Jesus walked among the nonbelievers, the poor and the crippled, the wretches of society," Dee said, arranging her ingredients on the shelf. "So I don't think we just need to surround ourselves with fellow Christians, right? We gotta get down there in the trenches to really do God's work."

I uttered a one-syllable word of agreement, but I was actually thinking about how if I spent any time in the trenches, I was quite sure I would be changed by the trenches, and not vice versa.

Cass did come to our apartment. And I couldn't help taking that as a sign, that maybe she had thought about me during the past week, the way I had been thinking about her. She showed up late, appearing in the doorway while we were eating our omelets. She brought a girl I'd never seen before and introduced her as "Ali . . . a friend." There were eight of us, all with plates in our hands, scattered throughout the living room. Most mumbled a hello, mouths full. I looked down at the massive blob on my plate. I had been rearranging the food, tearing apart the middle of the omelet so the meat and chopped peppers spilled out, a cascade of colors surrounded by thick chunks of yellow. I nodded hello to Cass. She smiled. I looked back at my plate, cutting the omelet again as if about to take a bite.

Dee quickly bounced out of her seat, playing both hostess and cook. Cass and Ali followed her into the little kitchen, and the three of them chatted while Dee cracked eggs and chopped more veggies. I waited two minutes, just long enough so it didn't seem like I was following them.

"Hey, hey," Dee said, sliding her spatula under the cooking eggs. "What can I do you for?" (Dee often did this, putting words slightly out of order, so you had to pause and process the full sentence.)

"Just getting some OJ," I lied. I excused myself past Ali and Cass and poured the juice into one of the red plastic cups that Dee had bought for easier cleanup. I leaned against the counter.

"So . . . how's it going?" I asked Cass, taking a sip of juice.

"It's good to see you again," she said, and didn't say anything else.

"It's good to see you," I eventually replied, after swallowing without choking. Dee glanced between the two of us, her eyebrows raised.

"Cass and I went to dinner together—" I paused and looked at Cass—"what was it, last week?"

"Last Thursday," Cass said.

"Gotcha," Dee said, returning her attention to the frying pan.

"Sasha was there, too," I added, as if Sasha's presence validated the dinner. As if otherwise I would later have to explain why I was spending time with an atheist—a gay atheist. When I flashed back to that night at BJ's, which I did often, Sasha played only a bit role, like she was a waitress floating in and out of the picture, a fuzzy character in contrast with me and Cass, the two of us shining in my mind's eye with ridiculous clarity. Maybe that's why I noted Sasha's presence, because I kept forgetting it myself.

Nobody said anything else for a second, so I lifted the red cup to my lips and took another sip of orange juice. "Dee makes a mean omelet," I said, then slipped out of the kitchen, back to my own plate of food, way out there in the living room, so far away from where I wanted to be. I sat down, shifting my chair a few degrees so I would be able to see the kitchen out of the corner of my eye without swiveling my neck completely. I took a few bites of food that I didn't taste. My teammates were talking about the game we had lost at Iowa State. Cass and Ali carried their food to a different corner of the living room, somewhere behind me that I couldn't see. I felt like I was facing away from a movie I really wanted to watch.

Less than an hour later, my teammates began excusing themselves. It was a rare day off from practice, and they wanted to relax in their own spaces. I high-fived them goodbye, then glanced at Cass, who was carrying her empty plastic plate to the kitchen. She dropped it into the garbage, then turned and watched as everyone left. She leaned against the wall of the kitchen's pass-through, seemingly waiting for something. Her left hip was jutting out, and she was wearing a button-down shirt that was open at the collar. She looked impossibly cool, and I remembered in a flash that I was impossibly not. Whatever I was feeling had to be a one-way street—needed to be a one-way street.

I collected a stack of discarded red cups and passed by her. She had just pulled something out of her back pocket and was flipping it open. "What's that?" I asked, pausing next to her.

"This is my gay wallet," she said, holding it between us. "I just got it from Urban Outfitters." The wallet was about the size of a credit card and had two bands, crossing, that pinned down her money and IDs. When she wanted to free something, she made a quick motion, like she was turning over a playing card, and the ID came loose, as if by magic. She used the same motion to secure the ID again. (To this day, whenever I see one of these wallets—and I see them a lot—I think of that moment, of standing next to Cass and asking her about her "gay wallet," feeling equal parts excited and scared shitless that I was so near to her. I will never buy one of these economical wallets because I don't want to have continual flashbacks to this feeling.)

"That's cool," I said stupidly, then walked away and threw the cups in the garbage.

Everyone except Cass and Ali had left. I could feel the clock ticking down, but I had no moves in my arsenal. Ali was sitting with Dee in the living room, and Ali was laughing because Dee could charm anyone. I was standing a few feet away from Cass and surveying the room to see if I could collect any more trash. Cass glanced down at her watch, then looked up at Ali. She opened her mouth to call to her friend, but then stopped. She turned to me, as if some irrepressible thought had just crossed her mind.

"How about hanging out later?" she asked.

"Yes," I said quickly, without even looking at her.

She laughed softly. "Does seven o'clock work? You have a car?"

I turned to her and said, "Yes, I do, and seven works."

She gave me her address, adding, "I figure this way we can keep talking about God, right?"

Before I could respond, Cass said to Ali, "You ready?"

Ali popped off the couch with a "Yup," and the two of them were gone a few seconds later, thanking Dee profusely on their way out the door.

I helped Dee clean the kitchen. We put everything back the way it was. My face felt flush, like I had been in the sun for a while. Dee stacked the final clean pan and draped the dishtowel on the handle of the oven. She yawned and said, "Nap time," stretching her arms over her head. As she walked down the hallway toward her room, she called back to me, "Let's leave for Bible study around five?"

She might as well have said, "Don't forget we're flying to Africa tonight"—that's how out-of-the-blue the Bible study reminder felt. I hadn't thought about this obligation since the moment Dee mentioned that Cass might be coming over.

"Sure," I said after a beat. "That sounds good."

I don't know what we talked about at Bible study. Chrissy probably took us through a lesson from our workbook, *Women of the Bible*, in which we tested our knowledge by filling in blanks such as this one: "Jesus cast _____ demons out of Mary Magdalene." (Answer: Seven! All those demons just disappeared. Poof!) Since we had left the apartment, leather Bibles in hand, my heart rate was holding steady at fifteen to twenty beats higher than normal.

By the time we pulled back into our complex, it was 6:45. I needed to go. I started walking with Dee, like I was heading inside, then peeled off to the right where my car was parked, making sure to dangle my keys so they jingled. Dee spun on her heel and asked, "Wait, where you going?"

I kept walking toward my car while answering, "I'm just meeting Cass for a coffee or something." I spun around and started walking backward, so I was facing Dee but still making progress toward my Honda. She had stopped and was watching me.

"Yeah, okay," she said. "So I guess I'll see you later?"

Feeling like I had just been released from a hook, I breezily replied, "Definitely! See you later, bud!"

And then I was in my car, zooming away.

—⁓—

Cass bounded out of her house before I could even put the car in park. I had arrived exactly at 7 p.m. because punctuality is the first lesson you learn when you play college sports. As I watched Cass jog to the car, her strides long and easy, an energy started to rise inside my chest. I wanted to pull the rearview mirror toward me so I could check my reflection, but I didn't want her to see me looking at myself. I ran my hand across my hair, which was pulled back, to make sure there weren't any significant bumps. Cass pulled open the passenger's side door and lowered herself into the seat. She was wearing jeans and a hoodie, and her hair was also pulled back, a puff of curls behind her head.

"Hey," I said, resting my hand on the gear shift.

"Hi," she said, smiling at me, temporarily breathless from the quick jog across the front lawn.

"Where to?" I slipped the car into first gear and eased us away from the curb.

"Let's go shoot baskets," she said, like she had wanted to do this very thing all along.

I turned toward her, surprised at the suggestion. "Yeah? Where?"

"Don't you know a good place?" she said, and I knew right away she meant the Coors Events Center, the 10,000-seat arena where we practiced and played our home games. I checked my keychain, which was dangling from the ignition, to make sure I still had keys to the arena, which I did.

"To the Events Center," I said, spinning the wheel so we completed a U-turn.

The entire arena was dark, and I knew, from late nights shooting by myself, that it would take a few minutes for the bulbs to slowly burn before we could see what we were doing. "This way," I said to Cass after I had flipped the switches. "The balls are back in the locker room." The lights had just started to hum as we walked down the hallway. We couldn't see much, only the outlines of the walls, which made me so much more aware of the things I could feel. I sensed the energy of Cass behind me. And I had never been more conscious of another human's presence—like a buzz, a radiation. I felt that if I got too close, she would be a magnet, and I would be pulled in.

We entered the locker room, and I quickly lifted two balls off the rack, which had been rolled just inside the door. I tossed one ball to Cass, tucked the other under my arm, and led us back out to the floor. Cass dribbled as we walked, finally saying, "I've been to a few games."

The overhead lights were casting a soft glow across the court, enough to see the baskets and each other. They would get brighter with each minute. As we stepped onto the wooden floor, raised two inches above the concrete, I said, "You've been to some of our games?"

Cass turned and pointed toward a corner of the arena, high up, and answered, "Me and some of the rest of us. The lesbians love women's basketball."

"Right," I said, because I knew this. I had just never allowed myself to process what it meant.

"We watch the games and discuss who on the team is gay," Cass said.

I lifted a soft shot toward the basket and watched as it went in, dropping cleanly through the net, the bounce of the ball echoing throughout the space. I didn't know how to respond to what she had just said, didn't really know what she meant. Did she think I was gay?

So I said what I thought was the truth: "Actually, nobody on the team is gay."

She dribbled in and made a layup, adding, "Well, it is women's basketball."

We spent the next half-hour taking shots and talking about where we grew up. Cass had grown up near Chicago and gone to Missouri State on a softball scholarship. But something about the place didn't feel right, and she loved the outdoors, so she transferred to Colorado without knowing a single person. Her family now lived in a suburb outside Dallas.

When we were done, I shut off all the lights, jogged to the locker room, put the balls on the rack, and then we walked to my Honda. Once we were both inside the car, I realized I didn't want to drop Cass off. I wanted to stay with her. "Maybe I'll take the long way back to your apartment?" I asked, looking at her and then away.

"Yes, do that," she said, and there was a lightness in her eyes.

As I was backing out of the parking spot, I swiveled my head to make sure no one was coming. Just then, I felt her hand on my neck. I tensed. I later wished I hadn't, wished I'd done something bolder and more in line with what my heart was telling me. But I froze. My shoulder blades pinched together, as if her touch was not at all what I wanted, and the air between us became thick. She left her hand there for a few minutes, then gently removed it.

"So tell me about what you believe," Cass said finally. And we kept driving, for an hour, maybe more, talking about God and life and beliefs and love. The night was black, but the moon hung high in the sky.

That ride was the first of many. On most nights, after I was done with basketball practice and she was finished with track, we would make some excuse to use my Honda, then drive through the back roads in the towns surrounding Boulder, talking and listening to CDs she had compiled, the songs becoming imprinted on my heart. Within a few weeks, although I would never admit this to Cass, I was in love with her. I know this now more than I knew it then, but during one of our rides, there was a distinct moment between us, and I can still hear her words clearly. I was letting her drive my car, and she was talking about her future, her hands gripped tightly to the wheel, like she was holding onto that very minute so it wouldn't pass so quickly. "I see myself in a city," she said. "I don't know, maybe New York, and I'm just walking down the street with the woman I love, holding hands." I know now that I must have loved her because I wanted to be that woman, and I was hoping desperately she was picturing us.

Of course, I said nothing in the moment. I had admitted to her that I was thinking of her all the time, even while in class, and she would smile because she knew what this really meant. I would tell her that how I felt was wonderful, and also confusing, but that I didn't necessarily believe I was gay. I told her I was simply excited about our burgeoning friendship, as all women are when they forge a new bond. I told her I believed my attraction to her was emotional, not physical, which was a clichéd cop-out, a way of wanting someone's time and love without committing your entire self. I imagine she recognized my mental gymnastics for what they were, the first steps of the coming-out process. And I imagine she hoped I would be strong and confident enough to plant my feet on the ground, to stop twisting away from my truth.

But my Christian teammates were perched on my shoulders, whispering, *This is just agape love.*

—⚹—

One morning, not long after the sun rose, I pulled myself out of bed and decided I needed to go running. I needed to clear my fuzzy head. I wasn't sleeping much because my mind was being eaten away by thoughts of Cass, followed by thoughts about how thinking of Cass meant something it couldn't mean. But how could love be wrong? A civil war had erupted inside my head, and my mind and body were exhausted from the conflict. Is there anything more tiring in this world than keeping yourself from loving someone? It's like working against gravity, muscles straining, clinging to the side of a mountain.

I put on a sweatshirt and sat on the edge of my bed to tie my sneakers. The rest of the apartment was quiet; Dee and Lindsay wouldn't be awake for another two hours. I gently closed the front door behind me. The morning was dewy, drips of water glistening at the end of green leaves. The sun was freed from the horizon, and birds were chirping, seemingly excited about the oncoming arrival of spring. The world, I noticed, seemed very sure of itself, not at all confused.

I didn't even stretch. I just started running toward the trail that connected at the back of the apartment complex. My sneakers crunched the pulverized gravel that lined the path. I breathed deeply, filling my lungs with the crisp air. All of a sudden, I decided I needed an answer: choose God or choose Cass. I ran harder, the thoughts flying through my mind as I sprinted the path, as I brushed past the leaves, as I dipped myself under extended tree branches. I turned around at the trail's end and ran even harder on the way back. I was playing a game of roulette, and everything depended on where my mind was when I stopped running. I flew across the bridge covering the creek that led to the back of our apartment, and I crossed my imaginary finish line. My chest was heaving. I felt alive.

I leaned down on my knees, a luxury Coach Barry did not allow us during practice because she said it would be a sign of weakness to our opponents if we did it during games. I gripped the tops of my knees and watched the sweat beads drip off my nose and form a pool in the dirt at my feet.

The decision was made. I would not be gay.

No, it was more than that: I was not gay. It seemed that simple, like choosing to turn off the light when exiting a room.

That afternoon, I called my mom between classes. I was walking past the CU library when I stopped at a common area, where many different walkways met and spilled out to the rest of the campus. There was a bench facing other benches, and I sat down. "Mom, good news," I told her, speaking into my new silver cell phone. "I'm not gay." I went on to explain how I had met this girl, she ran on the track team, and I had started contemplating that maybe I was gay. But I wasn't!

I had this conversation with the kind of bold self-assurance of someone who had made a definitive decision—Not Gay—and then somehow seemed to believe it was perfectly acceptable to commiserate with my mom over what a close call it had been. She sounded baffled on the other end of the line, saying things like, "What do you mean gay?" To which I responded, "Don't even worry about it now. All is good." She must have hung up from that call and stared at her phone, confused as hell. I hadn't been talking to my parents much because, well, what was there to say? This was unusual for us, as I typically called one of them, sometimes both, multiple times a day, just to say hi and tell them I loved them. I still loved them; I just needed every ounce of energy I possessed to get myself through each day. It felt like I was shuffling around inside of a body that I needed to inject with some kind of elixir so nobody would notice I wasn't me anymore.

That same night, I met Cass in the computer room at Dal Ward and we decided to go for a ride. I told her about my run, about the conclusion I had reached. I just wasn't gay—isn't that exciting? She raised her eyebrows, quickly, then made her face soft again. She nodded, the motion almost imperceptible at first, then deeper and more forceful as she began to accept what I believed to be true. She let the words sink deep into her heart and absorbed them fully, so that if later I wanted to remove them, I probably couldn't. Cass had been proudly gay for years, since high school, and she had little desire to go back to being scared and confused. She was not going to live in the closet again, for me or for anyone.

The next few days, a melancholy settled over me. At basketball practice, I would run up and down the court one time and my muscles would scream at me, exhausted, depleted, like they were tearing apart. I'd fold over on myself, gasping for breath. On more than one occasion, Dee came and stood next to me in between reps, leaning in to ask, "Are you okay? Talk to me, please." But what was there to say? Tell Dee I loved a woman and I was turning myself inside out?

I was driving home after one of those hard practices, and it was raining. I was glad for the weather, because it justified my melancholy, making the world seem sad, too. I exited off Diagonal Highway—we lived a few miles outside Boulder—and pulled into the gas station near the Safeway. After turning on the pump, I leaned against the car and tilted my head up toward the sky, squinting against the falling raindrops. I closed my eyes and heard the sound of a buzz, my cell phone vibrating in the cup holder. The gas tank clicked full, and I climbed back into the car.

The small LCD screen of the flip phone was bright: one new message. Not in the habit of texting, which seemed so complicated, I pulled open the phone and was surprised to see Cass was the sender. My eyes flew to the message: "Nothing worth having comes easily." I read it again and again, the rain swamping the windshield of the car, blurring the outside world. Eventually, I closed the phone and placed it back in the cup holder. The pain started in my core, a kind of vibration, until I could feel it choking me, filling my lungs. I let out a long, soft cry—*Ahhhhhhhhhh*—like a balloon running out of air. My eyes filled with heavy tears, so now my vision inside the car matched my view through the windshield. I leaned forward until my forehead was resting on the steering wheel. Then I started to sob uncontrollably, and didn't stop until my body was empty and sore.

I probably would have stayed there longer, but a car pulled in behind me and gently beeped, flashing its lights. I started my engine and gingerly drove back to my apartment, the wipers rhythmically thudding, left-right, left-right, left-right.

—∞—

"Hey, kid," Dee said, sounding chipper, as I trudged past the door of her room.

"Hey, hey," I said, trying to inject life into my voice and make the words sound light and airy.

They must have landed with a thud because Dee walked toward me and stood in the threshold of her door.

"Wait, what's wrong?" she asked.

I didn't turn around; my puffy face and bloodshot eyes would give me away. "I don't know yet," I said, walking into my room so she couldn't see me. "I'm trying to figure it out. Maybe I'll come see you in a little bit."

"Okay, kiddo."

I closed the door softly behind me, not wanting to make Dee feel like I was rejecting her. I leaned against the door and slid down it, wrapping my arms around my knees. Maybe I would sit like this the rest of the night, in a ball, literally holding myself together.

A minute later, I heard Dee's footsteps on the carpet. I could sense her presence on the other side of my door and pictured her debating whether or not to knock. Then she did, and I felt the vibration in my back, pinned against the wood. I quickly crawled to the edge of my bed and hoisted myself up, pretending I was untying my shoes.

"Yeah," I said, pulling at a lace. Dee peeked around the door and asked if she could come in. I nodded, and she closed the door behind her, taking one large stride, then lowering herself into my leather desk chair.

"Kater," she said, looking at me compassionately. She leaned forward and clasped her hands together. "You're falling apart on me. Please . . . will you talk to me?"

I nodded and said that I would. "Just give me a minute, okay? I don't know how to say this."

Dee leaned back and said, "Take as long as you need." She lifted one of the books off my desktop and started reading. We sat like this for a while. At some point I allowed myself to flop back on the bed, as if I just didn't have the energy to hold myself upright anymore. I crossed my hands behind my head and stared at the popcorn ceiling, a rough shade of white.

"I just . . ." I blurted out, not yet ready to finish the sentence, letting my voice trail off.

A few minutes later, I sat up again and looked at Dee. She was seemingly absorbed in her new book.

"Okay, I just . . ." I began again. She lowered the book a few inches and looked at me. "I just, well . . ." I stared down at the tops of my sneakers, willing myself to say it this time, finally. "I have feelings for Cass. And I'm sick about it because I know God doesn't approve of it. I don't know what to do."

Dee put the book back on the desk, in the exact spot she had found it. She didn't say anything for a minute, but I could tell by looking at her that she was processing what I had said, determined to respond in the exact right way.

"Everything is going to be fine," Dee said. "I've been thinking about this a lot lately, and I don't believe being gay is wrong. I think love comes from God—all love."

I inhaled sharply, and deeply, the first full breath I had taken in some time.

CHAPTER 10

"God Isn't Okay with You Being Gay"

When the knock came at my bedroom door, I wasn't asleep. I should have been. It was 3:48 a.m., and the digital numbers on my alarm clock seemed almost like a reprimand: Why aren't you sleeping? My mind was still drowning in thoughts. Now that my best friend was willing to stand by me, all of this became so much more real. What would I tell my parents? How would my teammates react? I wanted to see Cass, to tell her not to give up on me, that I would figure it out. I was lying on top of the covers, staring at the ceiling, the blandness of the view in contrast with the cacophony in my head. Each time I blinked, I opened my eyes and hoped that the morning—the real morning—had arrived.

I heard Dee in the room next to mine, opening and closing her drawers. I heard the creak of the one drawer that had needed fixing since we lived together as freshmen. It was at this point, with the sound carrying through the cardboard-thin walls, that I rolled over and stared at the clock by my bed and saw it was 3:48. When I closed my eyes, the red numbers were burned into the back of my eyelids. I heard a soft knock on my door. The wood was cheap and hollow (our ground-floor apartment cost each of us $333 a month), and the

noise seemed to get trapped inside the door and bounce around. I
said nothing because I wasn't sure what was happening. Why would
Dee need me at this hour? But a few seconds later, I heard a second
knock. There was no urgency in it; the sound was soft, the cadence
almost inquisitive.

"Yeah?" I said, hoping my voice was just loud enough to make it
through the door. I watched as the brass knob turned and Dee poked
her head inside.

"You awake?" she asked, because that's the kind of absent-
minded thing Dee would say. I ignored her question and sat up on
my bed, figuring that was answer enough.

"Can we go for a ride?" she asked. She still wasn't fully inside
my room—she was cut in half by the door—but I could see that she
was wearing her fleece jacket over a hooded sweatshirt. I looked
down and noticed her sneakers were tied.

I rubbed my eyes and nodded. "Give me two minutes."

"I'm going to heat up the car," she said, gently pulling the door
shut. I heard the metal knob slowly turn and latch, then I sat there
for a minute and listened as Dee walked down the hallway and out
the front door. A few seconds later, I heard the engine of her Jeep
Cherokee come to life in the parking lot.

Okay, this is really happening, I thought to myself. I stood and
walked to the door of my closet. I took my black Colorado jacket off
a hanger and pulled it on. Then I kneeled down and pushed my feet
into a pair of already-tied sneakers. I flipped my head upside down
and wrapped my long brown hair into an elastic band, swirling the
hair in on itself so it made a funky little bun, which is how I wore it
every day, including in practice and games. I wasn't surprised that
Dee wanted to go for a ride in the middle of the night—she was
spontaneous and passionate about life—but I was anxious to hear
what she might say, considering our conversation the night before.
I zipped up the front of my jacket as I walked down the hallway to

the front door, a wave of emptiness suddenly passing through me. I hadn't eaten much in weeks. The dark cold slapped me as I stepped into it, and I felt chilled to the bone, burying my chin further into my coat as I walked toward Dee's light gray car. I could see the red brake lights and the smoke chugging from the muffler. The door handle was covered in a film of ice. I tugged it open and slipped into the passenger seat. I had executed this move a thousand times before, but never with such a pit in my stomach.

Dee glanced at me and smiled weakly, then shifted the car into reverse and backed out of the spot, looking more intently into her rearview mirror than she probably needed, given that everyone around us was still asleep. I looked out my window and waited; this was her show, her turn to talk. The jeep's engine grumbled through the first mile, in protest of this ill-timed outing. The horizon was dark, the fields around us coated in thin ice. Dee cranked the heat, and I reached toward the dash to absorb it as soon as it was released from the vent.

"So . . ." Dee began at one point, but then trailed off, becoming preoccupied with a right-hand turn onto an empty road. A few minutes later she finally said what she came to say—and to her credit, she looked me in the eyes when she said it. The road ahead of us was straight, and no other cars were near. She put her left hand on the wheel at twelve o'clock, her right hand on the gear shift, and turned her body slightly toward mine, locking eyes.

"What I said last night was wrong," Dee stated firmly. "God isn't okay with you being gay."

She turned away first, eyes back on the road, but her body was still leaning toward mine, like a drawbridge slowly lifting. I withdrew my hands from the heat of the dashboard and wrapped them around myself until they were gripping the sides of my rib cage.

"I prayed about it all night," Dee continued. "I left your room and I went to the Bible for more answers. I read, and I prayed, and

I read some more—for hours. And God made it clear to me that the message I gave you was wrong, and I needed to tell you the truth."

"Okay," I said weakly, without moving, because I felt like I was made of glass.

"God won't support you in this," Dee said, her words like a thrown rock.

CHAPTER 11

Sleeping in the Locker Room

That semester, I had a class in Norlin Library, a place I didn't spend much time because athletes had so many academic resources of their own at Dal Ward. When I had made my recruiting visit to Colorado, one weekend in the fall of my senior year of high school, the coaches took me on a tour of the campus. One of the last stops was Norlin, an elegant building perched at the edge of the quad. At the time, the library's main entrance happened to be under renovation, so we stood in front of the imposing edifice, on the well-tended grass in front, and one of the coaches pointed out the inscription etched into the stone: ENTER HERE THE TIMELESS FELLOWSHIP OF THE HUMAN SPIRIT. There was a sign tacked up in wood underneath that phrase, one word spray-painted in red: "Closed."

We stayed there for a minute or two, laughing at the accidental comedy the university had created. And I thought of that moment—standing on the quad, laughing—every time I walked into the library. The "Closed" sign had long been removed, but I still read the inscription as: ENTER HERE THE TIMELESS FELLOWSHIP OF THE HUMAN SPIRIT . . . CLOSED.

The morning after my car ride with Dee—just a few hours later, actually—I forced myself to smile as I entered the library. I was wearing my CU basketball backpack, filled with my books, and I gripped the straps tightly, shuffling my feet, head down. I paused

at the threshold and glanced up at those words, adding "Closed" at
the end. The class I was taking, located in a room on the top floor
of Norlin, was not going well for me, which was an unfamiliar turn of
events. I had always been a good student, but since meeting Cass
just a few weeks into the spring semester, I had wandered through
the days with a far-away look in my eyes. My Library Sciences class
got the worst of it because it was at 1 p.m., my last class of the day.
By then my mind was twisted into knots, so I usually stared out the
room's oversized windows, eyes glazed, trying to untangle myself.
Other times, I wrote what I hoped were witty notes to Cass, trying
desperately to make her laugh, trying so hard to compensate for my
greatest flaw: weakness. Making matters worse, the professor clearly
had no patience for athletes, as I had missed a couple of classes
traveling to away games, and she had warned me that I couldn't miss
any more sessions, for any reasons, including university-sanctioned
athletic events.

I walked up the magnificent staircase to the top of Norlin,
gripping the wooden handrail as it swirled around, above the students
scurrying from one place to another. I entered the open-spaced
classroom and took the seat at the very end of the long wooden table
that served as our meeting place. Our professor sat in a different seat
each class, as we all gathered around what seemed like a medieval
banquet table. The light from the windows poured into the space.
Having arrived a few minutes early, I crossed my arms on the table
and rested my head—a catnap, I told myself. I fell asleep instantly.

The professor announced the start of class by dropping her stack
of folders and books onto the table, and then slipped into the seat
directly across from me. I raised my eyes, feeling exhausted and
dazed. My face was puffy. She cut me a look of disapproval, then
craned her neck down the table—all of the seats were filled—
and launched into that day's lesson. The room was warm from the
sunlight, and I started thinking about the last time I had fallen asleep
at night and not woken up until morning. How long had it been?

A month? My eyelids were getting heavy, my mind drifting, going somewhere without fear or judgment, like a peaceful beach with the waves lapping. My head bobbed and my eyes flashed open. I glanced around, but nobody was looking at me. Nothing to see here, people! I put my elbow on the table and rested my chin on my palm, then thought better of that position because I would have been asleep in a few seconds. I leaned back in my chair and crossed my arms across my chest. What was the professor saying? Her mouth was moving, she was looking around the table at all of the students, who seemed to be pulling out notebooks and opening to empty pages. I thought about how I should lean down into my backpack and do the same, but I couldn't make my limbs move. My eyes closed and my chin dipped.

"Hey!" I heard fingers snapping. "Heeelllllloooooo! I'm talking to you!"

My eyes flew open. The professor was holding her hand over the table, a few inches from my face. Her reading glasses were at the edge of her nose, threatening to jump. She withdrew her arm and fell back into her seat, shaking her head in disgust.

"Is this nap time for you?"

Her voice was laced with disdain. I wanted to shake my head, to try to explain myself, but years of playing basketball had taught me to listen and accept criticism, to believe these moments were rhetorical. If you wanted them to end quickly, you said nothing. So I waited.

"Do you think this information doesn't apply to you because of that gear you're wearing?" She gestured toward my outfit, a gray, team-issued sweatshirt and matching sweatpants. "I'm tired of you checking out each time you walk into this room," she said. "Get it together."

The professor turned to the rest of the students, as if they were her co-conspirators and all felt the same way about my half-assed performance in Library Sciences. "Anyway," she said to them, flipping through the open book in front of her, "where were we?"

I reached into my backpack at my feet and took out my notebook. Then I sat up taller in my chair and scooted it closer to the table. I felt the burn of embarrassment, but the tears caught me by surprise. A few of them dripped onto the open page, blotting the notes that I had scribbled in blue ink during previous classes. When I saw them fall, I had a split second of wondering where the water had come from. Perhaps there might be a leak in the roof or a broken pipe? I reached my right hand to my eyes, surprised to feel how wet they were. Then I moved my hand to my brow, cupping my fingers over my eyes while planting my elbow on the table.

So much is about framing, about context. This professor did not know anything about me except for what she saw during one hour every Monday, Wednesday, and Friday. And what she saw was a lazy, apathetic, unfocused student who, in her estimation, felt immune to academic pressure because of her standing as an athlete. From her perspective, I was acting superior and demeaning the very thing she was passionate about. Of course, if she had pulled me aside and asked a simple question—Are you okay?—she would have realized I wasn't lazy at all, but rather, at that moment, I was having my ass handed to me by life. To this day, when I'm preparing to deem someone lacking or Not Good Enough, I try to remember that moment and realize that occasionally someone's best is being spent on something more important, something inside herself, and not the thing you're currently engaging her in—so rarely do our priorities match.

I kept my eyes down and finished out the hour, repeatedly wiping away tears. I didn't want the professor to see me crying because the tears weren't for her. I leaned across my notebook and wrote every word she uttered, filling four or five lined pages. She said nothing to me as I packed up my things and left the classroom.

I walked across campus to the Coors Events Center. Practice started at 3:30. When I got there, I walked into the training room, into the supply closet, where the tape and gauze were stored, and grabbed a chewy Power Bar. After eating half of it, I lay down on the padded training table and took a nap, using my backpack as a pillow, waking up only when I heard my teammates streaming down the hallway to the locker room, laughing and joking about their day. We were in the homestretch of the season. We had two games left in the regular season before we traveled to Dallas the following week for the Big 12 tournament. Immediately following tomorrow's practice, we would fly to Lincoln, Nebraska, to play the Cornhuskers. We were good. Although we had lost a few games recently, we were still ranked in the Top 20 nationally and were a lock to get a bid in the upcoming NCAA tournament.

I changed into my practice gear—black mesh shorts and a reversible black mesh top—laced up my ankle braces and sneakers, and walked out to the floor almost an hour before the start of practice. I sat in the first row of the stands and put my feet on the silver metal railing. The managers walked in and out, first rolling out the rack of balls, then carrying out the big pad that the coaches would use to mimic contact from an opponent as we finished drills going to the basket. One of the managers spotted me and cocked his head.

"All good?" he asked.

"All good," I lied.

Usually there was nothing more reassuring to me than an empty gym, the space reminding me that I could shape my own destiny, could fill the gym with my work and sweat and become exactly the player I intended to be. That was true for basketball, anyway. But this supposed internal flaw in my character—I could not shape it to be something else, because it seemed to be implanted whole inside me, in a place I couldn't reach without pouring out the rest, like emptying a bottle of tequila to see if there is a worm. How much of myself was I willing to waste?

When my first teammate walked onto the floor and grabbed a basketball off the rack, I stood from my seat in the stands and joined her. Sitting there any longer would warrant repeated inquiries of how I was doing, and was I all right? Halfway through practice, I found myself standing at midcourt during a break, taking a pull of water from the green Gatorade bottle on the sideline. I lodged it back in its holder and then stared out at the court, hands on hips, shoulders sagging, elbows fluttered out, like a deflated super hero. One of the assistants broke away from the coaching huddle at midcourt (the coaches often gathered during water breaks) and made her way toward me. She tilted her head as she approached, then draped an arm across my shoulder. We leaned against the scorer's table.

"Are you okay?" she asked, and I saw there was a pained look in her eyes. I didn't say anything, so she continued. "Something seems off with you for the last few games or so, like your mind is elsewhere."

"Has everyone noticed?" I asked, nodding my head toward the coaching circle.

"We're just worried about you," she said, answering the question without really answering it.

"I'm just having a tough time lately," I said.

"Want to talk about it?"

"I don't think I can."

The two of us stood like that for a few more seconds, until Coach Barry blew the whistle announcing the restart of practice. When we pushed ourselves off the scorer's table, my coach slapped me on the back and said, "Whatever it is, hang in there, Kate. We need you."

I told her I would try my best.

—⚏—

I showered quickly after practice and tucked myself back into my sweats. My hair was still wet; I could have squeezed water out of it when I flipped it up into a bun. I was quick in everything I did, so I was one of the first out of the locker room. Dee, on the other hand, was slow in everything she did, dripping along like honey being poured, as if time would never end. I stopped in the training room on the way out to talk books with Kristen, our trainer. We both loved to read, and we had started our own little book club of sorts, except we didn't actually read the same books at the same time; we just talked about the ones we liked, some of them overlapping, some not.

"I need a good book recommendation," I said to Kristen, who was tidying up the room, stacking rolls of tape and wiping down the counters. I hopped up on the training table and let my legs dangle off the side. I had been treading water in the opening pages of the book I was currently trying to read. I blamed the book itself, when in reality my concentration was the problem. My mind wandered constantly, so that I had read the same three pages dozens of times, unable to inhabit the world the author was trying to create.

"What about the book you're reading now?" Kristen asked.

"I just can't get into it."

"That's unlike you," she said, closing the door to the utility closet.

"Yeah, I guess it is. Should I keep trying? You've read this one, right?"

"It gets good around page fifty," she said.

"Then I need to keep trying."

Dee walked into the training room with Lindsay. They stood in the doorway, pausing on their way out of the arena.

"Hey," Dee said to me. "We're headed home. You coming with?" She said this like it was any other day, like she had done a hundred times before, as if I would just pop off the training table and wave a carefree goodbye to Kristen.

"Nah, I'm good," I said. "I have a few errands to run."

Dee didn't press the issue. She just asked, "So we'll see you later?" But it wasn't rhetorical; she wanted to know.

"Yeah, catch you later," I replied, being careful not to define exactly when "later" might be. Lindsay gave Dee a confused look— she had no idea what was happening with me—then they disappeared from the doorway.

I sat there talking to Kristen about books until all of my teammates had left the arena. Finally she shut off the light inside her office, lifted her workbag, and motioned for me to walk her out. She turned off the overhead lights in the training room and locked the doors behind her. She didn't seem to think my behavior unusual, or if she did, she didn't give any indication of it.

"Don't give up yet on the book," she said, tossing her bag into the backseat of her Subaru and opening the driver's side door. "It's totally worth it."

"I won't," I answered, walking to my own car. "See you tomorrow."

I reached the door of my Honda as Kristen honked her horn on the way out of the parking lot. I acted like I was inserting the key into the door and watched as her taillights disappeared down the road. Once I was sure she was gone, I turned around and walked back into the arena. I dropped my book bag onto the carpet in the locker room and belly-flopped onto the black leather couch. I stayed like that for a few seconds, as if I'd been shot in the back and fell where I landed, then flipped myself over and stared up into the darkness, waiting for my eyes to adjust. The room gradually began to take shape; first, the framed pictures hanging over my head, featuring our basketball program's best teams; then, the outline of the dozen stools, sitting like little chess pieces in front of our lockers; and finally, the plush CU emblem emblazoned in the middle of the carpet. I laced my fingers behind my head and began thinking.

Be Gay. Or Be Christian.

If I was gay, I would become an outcast, someone to be whispered about. Just that fall I had hosted a recruit, a guard we really wanted to come play for CU. She was on her official visit to campus, and Coach Barry had put me in charge of her for the weekend, to introduce her to the team, answer her questions, make her fall in love with the Colorado Buffaloes. On the final day of her visit, I had joined the coaching staff as they gave the player and her mother a tour of the Coors Events Center. At one point, the coaches excused themselves—they were going to program the scoreboard to announce the player's name and number—and the recruit lifted a ball off the rack and walked onto the court, dribbling. I found myself sitting alone on the bench with her mother.

"I have a question," the woman said, clutching her purse tightly to her chest. She looked around to make sure no one else was in earshot.

"Anything," I said, because I really thought I could answer anything.

She leaned into me and said, "The other teams recruiting my daughter have mentioned that CU might be hiding a dirty little secret . . ."

"Okay," I prompted her, after she trailed off. She seemed to think we were on the same wavelength, which was not the case.

She leaned in closer, and I could see the exact shape of her earrings: they were small crosses, with a shiny little aqua jewel at the center of each one. "I'm asking if there are any dykes on the coaching staff," she said. "I don't want my daughter coming to a school run by dykes."

I instinctively leaned back against the cushioned chair, as if I had just played the most exhausting game of my life. "Wow," I said.

She appeared anxious for my response.

"All I can tell you is that the coaching staff here is amazing," I said. "They are disciplined and professional, and they care about each of us."

She waved her hand, pushing my words aside. "But there are no men on the staff," she said, incredulous, like she had uncovered a damning clue, the smoking gun, the bloody knife. "Not one."

I had not thought of this before, that No Men might be an important fact to some people. To me, it meant we had four extremely qualified women coaching us, all of whom had played Division I basketball. To this mother, it meant our coaches must hate men, and that they probably wanted to turn all of us players into disgusting, man-hating lesbians, too.

"Our staff is awesome," I said, which really wasn't answering her question about why we didn't have any men. I shrugged. "If I had to do it all over again, I would choose Colorado again."

She leaned back now, unsatisfied, still clutching her pocketbook tightly. The coaches appeared from around the corner a few seconds later, all of them pointing up at the scoreboard to show this woman what it would look and sound like if her daughter's name was announced in the starting lineup.

As I was lying atop that black leather couch in the locker room, I also pictured Cass and allowed myself to feel the excitement that ignited my senses whenever the thought of her entered my mind.

Or be Christian.

I draped my hand over the side of the couch and rummaged through my backpack. I pulled out my leather Bible and held it with both hands, lifting it up in front of me as if it were Baby Simba. Then I rested it on my chest. If God wanted me to reject myself, he would need to do something spectacular to make his wishes for me known.

I fell asleep a few minutes later.

CHAPTER 12

Lincoln, Nebraska

The next day's practice was short, and afterward Coach Barry reminded us that the bus would pull away from the arena thirty minutes later, at exactly 5:30. We had a quick commercial flight to Nebraska that evening. (We'd flown private charters my first two seasons, but that changed in 2001, when one of the planes carrying the Oklahoma State men's basketball team crashed while flying home after a game in Boulder. Coach Barry disliked our small propeller planes even before that tragedy; afterward, we switched to commercial jets.) As I was leaving the locker room, my team bag slung over my shoulder, Dee caught up with me and we walked together in silence to the bus, placing our bags in the storage underbelly, then finding our seats at the back. None of us had assigned seats, but each player laid claim to a specific row in which she always sat. I slid into mine. Dee was a row in front of me. She sat, then leaned her head around the corner.

"I didn't hear you come back last night," she said.

"Yeah," I answered, reaching into my backpack for my CD player and headphones. I placed the headphones around my neck, hoping they would be a clear signal that I didn't want to talk. Dee frowned, the look in her eyes earnest. I opened my eyes wide and flashed them quickly from left to right, like, *Yes, can I help you?*

She disappeared a few seconds later, both of us facing forward, watching everyone else stream onto the bus.

—⁓—

Whenever we played in Lincoln, we stayed at The Cornhusker, an elegant downtown hotel (despite its name). That night, we lugged our bags into the lobby. All twenty of us—coaches, players, support staff—were dressed head-to-toe in black Colorado gear. We contrasted sharply, in color and allegiances, with the red Nebraska décor inside the hotel. Colorado and Nebraska were bitter rivals back then, before the frenzy of conference realignment sent the Buffaloes to the Pac-12 and the Cornhuskers to the Big Ten (which of course has twelve teams, too, because the sports world is crazy like that).

As she did at every hotel, our director of basketball operations, Kris, checked all of us in and collected a stack of keycards. She distributed them and reminded us that dinner was in the downstairs conference room in fifteen minutes. I took my keycard with a quick bow—*Thank you, Kris*—and walked with my sophomore teammate, Vanessa, to our room. We dropped off our bags, washed our hands, and quickly made our way to the downstairs conference room. If the hotel staff had inadvertently put out pads of butter, the best strategy for snagging them was to arrive before Coach Barry did. Of course, it's not like I was spending any time thinking about hoarding butter that night, but I could tell that Vanessa was ready for adventure.

Half of the team was already there when we arrived. Vanessa looked from face to face, but each teammate cast her eyes downward, solemnly shaking her head. The message was clear: there would be no clandestine butter tonight. Still hopeful, Vanessa walked past the food table, peering in the crevices behind the large silver serving dishes. A minute later, she plopped down in the seat next to me, deflated.

"No butter," she said.

"Bummer," I replied, then spent a quick second marveling at the trifling problems that had previously occupied my brain space.

The coaches and support staff arrived a minute later, signaling the start of dinner. Kris sat next to Coach Barry. We were arranged in the shape of a square, with four long tables connected at the corners like dominoes. I looked at Kris, and my stomach did a back flip. She was the only openly gay person I knew besides Cass. She lived just outside of Boulder with her partner, and they occasionally hosted team functions together.

I nibbled my way through half a breast of grilled chicken and a few bites of salad. Toward the end of dinner, Coach Barry stood at her seat, as she often did. "Tomorrow is an important game for us," she said, tenting her fingers on the table in front of her, as if shielding two eggs from harm. "We have had a strong season, no doubt, but we need to continue improving as we head toward postseason play. Nebraska has a gritty, determined team, and they'll be amped up to play us."

Coach Barry wrapped up her speech a minute later, saying, "Now everyone get a good night's rest, and let's get back to Boulder with a victory." We all had listened to enough speeches to know the inflection in her voice when she finished, and we popped from our seats the second after we heard "victory," seemingly ready to give her a standing ovation. Instead, we filed out of the conference room, the decibel level rising as we jumped back into our conversations.

"Go ahead without me," I said to Vanessa. "I have a quick meeting."

Vanessa jogged a few steps to catch up with another group of teammates and didn't look back.

Kris and Coach Barry were still standing near their dinner table, and I lingered in the doorway, hiding like an amateur spy, waiting for them to leave. They walked out a different exit, and I tracked them from the adjacent corridor. At a crossroads in the hallways, they said goodnight and split off into separate directions. I followed Kris, injecting my stride with energy in order to catch up.

"Kris," I shouted in a whisper, desperate not to have Coach Barry, or anyone else, hear me.

Kris turned around and said, "Kate Fagan," using my full name, as she often did. "How may I help you?"

We were obviously alone in the hallway, but I did a quick scan to double-check. "What are you up to?" I asked.

Kris was about my height, but rail-thin with sharp elbows—like if you tried to guard her, you'd end up with dozens of little bruises. She had short brown hair that she has since grown out.

"I was just about to call it a night," she said, pointing upward, in the general direction of her room.

"Yeah, okay, um . . ." I stammered. I hadn't thought carefully about what I wanted to say to her, but whatever it was, I needed to be somewhere different than in this exposed hallway. "Can we talk?" I blurted out.

Now Kris did her own quick glance around to see if anyone was coming. "Absolutely we can talk," she said, making a motion toward somewhere else, like she had a place in mind, and I was grateful she had intuited that I didn't want to chat in the hallway. We walked to the lobby and climbed a staircase that led to additional common space on the second floor, overlooking the expanse of the entryway. Tucked into the corner were two overstuffed, floral print chairs, facing one another. Kris pointed to them, and I nodded—perfect.

As soon as we had settled into our chairs, I blurted out, "I think I'm gay."

Kris leaned forward. "Talk to me," she said.

"What's there to say?" I replied, a throwaway line, because I had a million things to say.

Kris made a sound of disbelief, then prompted me with questions. "Did you meet someone? How long has this been going on? Is it the first time you've considered this?"

I inhaled deeply, then slowly let out the air, looking up and away from Kris, the universal sign for *Oh Woe Is Me*.

That's when she realized something else—the other piece of this puzzle—and said, "Oh, wait. What does Dee think about this? And your FCA friends? Uh oh."

"Yeah," I said. "It's not good. Dee is the only one who knows. Well, and now you know, too."

Kris smiled and said, "Thank you for that, for trusting me."

I nodded, then added, "Please don't talk to anyone about this. I don't even know which way is up, yet."

"Of course."

"Thanks," I said. "Anyway, so, at first Dee seemed cool with it. We had a great talk the other night, and I was so relieved. But then a few hours later, in like the middle of the night, she woke me up to go for a car ride, and she went back on everything she said earlier. She told me, and I quote, 'God is not okay with you being gay.'"

Kris grimaced, as if the words were a physical blow. "That's not good," she said.

"Yeah, so it's been really hard lately," I continued. "I can't eat, I can't sleep, I can't think about anything. My mind is like this really crowded, jumbled place. It's starting to scare me."

"I know exactly what you mean," Kris said, nodding. "Also, this explains a lot."

"Explains what?"

She smiled again. "Why you've been so checked out lately during games and practices."

I dropped my eyes. "I know, I know," I said. "I feel like I'm playing underwater or something. I'm an embarrassment."

"You'll break out of it," Kris said, then flashed a conspiratorial grin, like we were finally getting to the good stuff. "So did you meet someone? Is that what happened?"

I told her everything I could about Cass, including how I felt the moment she walked into BJ's, as if it were the opening scene in a book, one I had never wanted to read but now I was hooked from the start. Kris asked me if it was the first time I had felt this way, and I admitted it wasn't. "But I didn't know what it meant before," I said. "You know? I just told myself that's the way everyone feels when building a new friendship. I think deep down I knew that was total bullshit, but there was no reason to address it. Now here comes Cass, who is openly gay—can you believe I fell for the most openly gay person on the entire campus?!—and her simple presence in my life doesn't allow me to hide behind that 'friendship' smokescreen anymore." (I made air quotes when I said "friendship.")

Kris asked me if Derek knew. I told her he didn't, but that I was going to break up with him. I told her I would gradually tell the people in my life, but I wasn't ready to come out yet—like the big Coming Out. And certainly not to my parents, whose reactions I couldn't even begin to predict. Actually, what I wanted most was to invite a few certain people to join me inside my closet.

"I'm not sure if that will be enough for Cass," I said. "I don't think she wants to be seeing someone closeted, even partially."

"I get that," Kris said. "It's tough. It's even hard for me to be fully out, although obviously I am, because women's college athletics is so paranoid and closeted."

I didn't say anything, hoping she would continue. She did. "It's just that this is a business about recruiting, first and foremost, and being gay isn't something parents want to hear about, or talk about, or even know—on any level."

I told Kris about my conversation that fall, the one with the mother of our recruit. "Did you tell Coach Barry what happened?" she asked. I said I hadn't, because, well, what exactly would I say? I felt like I would be crossing an invisible line, talking about things that weren't supposed to be talked about.

"What works for a lot of these coaches is being gay only on their own time," Kris said. "They just surround themselves with a small circle of people they trust. Those are the people who know who they really are. The rest of the time, they just hide that part of themselves."

As I listened, I thought to myself, *Huh . . . that sounds like a good compromise.*

CHAPTER 13

The Grassy Knoll

I walked into the Dal Ward weight room hoping to get a minute with Cass. I was leaving for Dallas, for the Big 12 tournament, following practice that afternoon. I hadn't heard from her since receiving her text message, and I knew it was my turn to act. I wanted to see her before I left because I could be gone as long as a week, depending on how many games we won.

The track team's lifting session was just ending. Cass was standing near the cubicles, pulling a hoodie over her head. She was laughing with a teammate standing next to her. She seemed so carefree, happy, easygoing, and I was reminded how long it had been since I felt that same way. When had I last laughed like that? She turned around and I caught her eye. She seemed surprised to see me, which made sense because I had my own practice, across campus, in only forty-five minutes. I raised my pointer finger indicating how much of her time I was requesting, then nodded to the door. There was a glass atrium between the main entrance to the weight room and the actual space where we lifted. In this atrium existed all of the trophies the Colorado Buffaloes had won over the years, including the football team's national championship in 1990. But the main attraction, inside a glass box in the middle of that narrow room, was the Heisman Trophy won by running back Rashaan Salaam in 1994.

Cass appeared a minute later, a quizzical look on her face. We were the only two people in the atrium, but we could be seen by everyone inside the weight room and in the main lobby of Dal Ward. I tried to make the feeling disappear, but I was worried what people might think if they saw us in there together, talking. I was convinced they could tell something existed between us, that the pull I felt toward her radiated out to everyone who passed.

"We're leaving for Dallas after practice," I said, as if this alone explained my presence.

She shrugged, which made my heart hurt. "Okay . . ." she said, waiting for me to explain more.

I was about to say what I had come to say, which was that I had been stupid to not realize my feelings sooner, and that I really, really liked her. I was about to ask her not to give up on me, because I was going to figure it all out. But just before I could say these things, Sasha walked through the door. Instinctively, I took a step back from Cass, which was ridiculous because we weren't even standing that close together. Sasha seemed hurried, but she paused and looked back and forth between us, and suddenly I felt desperate to fill the silence, to explain why I was standing there talking to Cass. Who knows what Sasha might think if I didn't tell her what to think.

"Hey, I was just coming to get a protein shake before practice," I said to Sasha. "And I ran into Cass."

Why was I lying? The words felt like nails in my mouth. I spit them out. I did not look at Cass, did not want to see her reaction.

The words seemed meaningless to Sasha. She put her hand on the door to the weight room and said, "I forgot my backpack here earlier—gotta grab it." Then she was gone.

"Have a safe trip to Dallas," Cass said, as she caught the door going back into the weight room before it had even fully closed behind Sasha.

I put the heel of each hand to my eyes and stood there like that for a long moment, inside my personal darkness. Sasha reappeared, now wearing her backpack, and I followed her toward the exit. As she held open the door for me, she said, apropos of nothing, "God is good."

This, of course, was not at all what I had been thinking.

—⁂—

By luck of the draw, I was rooming with Dee in Dallas; we hadn't been placed together on the road since the previous season. Dee and I rarely engaged in meaningless dialogue, but now a gulf existed between us, and the only bridge that still connected was paved with trivialities: the weather (hot in Dallas), practice (easy today, wasn't it?), and other superficial observations (this hotel is brand new!). Gone were the long talks about life and our futures and the meaning of God. It was like, without even discussing it, we had both agreed to this new kind of friendship, like we were two little old ladies out for lunch, filling the space between us with easy-to-digest tidbits.

Before bed the first night, Dee was getting ready to brush her teeth and she asked me what brand of toothpaste was my favorite. We hadn't said anything to each other for more than an hour. I had been reading (a novel) on my bed; Dee had been reading (the Bible) on hers. So maybe she just felt like saying words out loud to me, regardless of their content or worthiness. These particular words sounded especially empty. I lowered my book and looked at her, to see if she was seriously asking this question or if it was meant to be ironic, a nod to how ridiculously insignificant our interactions had become. She was standing over the bathroom sink, reading the fine print on her own tube of toothpaste. She appeared serious.

"Colgate," I said. "I only use Colgate. Because that's where my parents went to college."

When I was a little kid, there was a short period of time when I was embarrassed on behalf of my parents that their school shared a name with a brand of toothpaste. It seemed to demean their education, as other kids laughed at the maroon shirts I wore emblazoned with the Colgate University insignia. My classmates called it "Toothpaste U." But once I got older, I realized my fears were unfounded and that many people understood what a great little liberal arts school Colgate was—in addition to being toothpaste.

This quick interaction between me and Dee underscored how far we had fallen. I stood from my bed, pulled on my sweatshirt, and excused myself. "Going for a quick walk," I said.

Dee came out of the bathroom, her toothbrush dangling from her mouth, and she looked at the digital clock on the side table. She didn't say anything, just looked at the time, then at me, then back at the time.

"I have seventeen minutes," I said, letting her know I understood that I was cutting it close to curfew. Satisfied, she returned to the bathroom and closed the door behind her. I put my cell phone in my pocket and left. I walked the hallways for sixteen minutes, glancing at my phone a dozen times, hoping my dedication would produce a text, or a call, from Cass. But my phone stayed silent, like it wasn't a phone at all, just a heavy watch I carried in my pocket.

I returned to our room at exactly 10:59 p.m. I opened the door slowly, stepping into a pitch-black space because Dee had pulled shut the heavy window curtain. I could see the outline of a mound on her bed and hear her faint snores. Dee could fall asleep quicker than anyone I knew—pretty much the only thing she did fast—as if the world and its problems could be shut out just by closing her eyelids, which were apparently the equivalent of that heavy curtain. I slipped into my bed and pulled the covers over my head. I flipped open my cell phone one last time, illuminating the space underneath, like a little kid staying awake too late. No messages. I let the phone drop onto the bed. I curled into a ball and hoped for sleep.

We won our first game in the Big 12 tournament, guaranteeing we would be in Dallas another two nights. The evening after the win, I took an Ambien for the first time in my life. It was one of two that Kristen, the trainer, had given me earlier that year when I scheduled back-to-back late-night flights so I could squeeze in an interview for a summer internship in New York City, at NBC's *Late Night with Conan O'Brien*. I had flown overnight from Denver to New York's JFK airport, taken the subway to Rockefeller Center for the quick meeting, then had an early dinner with my sister, who had just graduated from Dartmouth and was working at Goldman Sachs on Wall Street. I was on the last flight back to Denver that night, which meant I would have only a few hours to sleep before morning classes, so Kristen had offered the Ambien to make sure I got enough rest to practice effectively that day and not be a zombie for our game the following night. But I didn't actually need sleeping pills at the time, because I was much more like Dee, a sleep monster. I gobbled sleep whenever and wherever: on the training table, on the plane, in the boarding area. All those 5 a.m. wakeup calls during preseason training, the early morning lifting and running sessions, had apparently left me permanently behind on my sleep, and I could usually drift off if you left me alone for more than a few minutes.

After our team dinner that night in Dallas, inside yet another soulless conference room, Kris had caught up with me as we walked out. She smiled and whispered, "How's Cass?"

I touched the pocket of my warm-up outfit, where my cell phone was making the fabric dangle, feeling more like a rock than a useful tool. "I don't know," I said softly. "I haven't heard from her."

Kris frowned for a second, then said, "That's okay; she knows you're busy."

I conceded the point to Kris without actually believing the excuse. She patted me reassuringly on the back and added, "Can't wait to meet her."

That's when I decided I needed to take the Ambien. Looking back, I now know my big mistake was taking the pill so early in the night. I walked directly back from the team dinner, rifled through my bag, and found the orange-tinted plastic medicine bottle. I shook it, and the two little pills danced around inside. It wasn't even 6 p.m. yet. Dee was gone from the room, as she had been for sizeable chunks of the trip, studying her Bible in various locations. I imagined spotting her in discrete little spots throughout Dallas—her head bowed, absorbing God's word—like I was playing a version of Where's Waldo. I went to the bathroom and filled a glass with tap water. I took the phone out of my pocket (still no messages) and tossed it across the room onto my bed. It bounced once near the pillows, awkwardly, and for a second I thought I might have miscalculated and the stupid thing would fly into the nightstand and break. When it came to rest on the corner of the mattress, I wasn't sure if I was relieved or disappointed.

I popped open the pill bottle and shook an Ambien into my left hand; it was so small it looked as if it had magically shrunk in my palm. I stared at myself in the mirror. I put my right hand up to the glass, blocking out my face, like in that famous Magritte painting— "The Son of Man"—with the apple covering his features. I dropped my hand after a minute and walked out of the bathroom, then sat on the edge of the bed and put the pill on my tongue, taking a gulp of water and tossing the liquid down my throat like it was bourbon from a tumbler. I swallowed, then flopped back on the bed, utterly exhausted and totally defeated.

I was asleep a few minutes later. I remember Dee drifting in and out of the room for the rest of the night, looking at me curiously because I was still in my travel suit and sneakers, atop the covers, curled around my cell phone as if someone might be coming to take it from me. When I awoke the next morning, nearly thirteen hours later, I felt guilty, like I had cheated, crossed some line I knew better than to cross. I felt guilty because I knew that God disapproved of drinking, at least in amounts that altered reality (which for college students was really the only kind of drinking), and I assumed he felt the same way about pills. I had always been especially careful about drinking and drugs—meaning I didn't do either—because of how strongly my Christian teammates felt about these "worldly temptations." And also because my mother's father had been an alcoholic, and I was paranoid about what that might mean for my own genetic makeup.

Worldly temptations were serious biz for the God squad. In fact, the opening act of the Christian Revolution on our team—our equivalent of the Boston Tea Party, when the scales tipped and a full-fledged movement was born—occurred at a house party. Or, more accurately, at a house that was supposed to host a party. It happened two years earlier, and we had just lost in the second round of the NCAA tournament. All five juniors on the squad, including Sasha, Lisa, and Kelly, lived together off campus with the only senior, Sammy. Six of them lived in a split-level home. Carrie and Cindy shared the ground floor with Sammy, while Sasha, Lisa, and Kelly shared the basement level, a dank space split into three rooms. (In retrospect, it must have been in this cave, dark and musty, that their faith blossomed, because just the previous year Lisa and Kelly had been regular college students, occasionally drinking and partying on the weekends and never mentioning to anyone how disappointed Jesus would be if we consumed a few Crown and Cokes and shots of Jagermeister.) So the day after our tourney loss, all of the other members of the team went to this house, intending to drink away our sorrows. But when we pushed through the front door, we felt a wave of tension that we could not immediately locate or define. The living room was to the left, lined with large couches, and the galley kitchen was straight ahead, boxes of beer and handles of liquor loading the counters, all unopened, seemingly intended for some other party, at some other location, awaiting transport. There were seven of us who had driven over from the dorms. We tiptoed into the living room and plopped down on the couches, looking back and forth at one another, our ears perked.

After a few minutes, we heard someone come up from downstairs and the door close behind her. Then Carrie appeared in the living room, shaking her head. She made it about halfway through before stopping, turning around, and walking back to the basement door. She opened it quickly and called down, "This is our house, too! You can't just make rules and expect us all to follow them!" She shut the door again.

It was like we were watching the opening act of a play. Carrie reappeared and sat on the far loveseat, letting out a long exhale. She didn't say anything for a minute, and we all looked at her, expectantly.

"Well, the downstairs crew doesn't want us 'serving drinks to minors' inside this house," Carrie said after a minute, mocking the phrase by dramatically enunciating each word: *serving . . . drinks . . . to . . . minors . . .*

Sammy appeared from the back hallway and joined us in the living room. "It's been a long night," she said, glancing at her watch, tapping the plastic face with her finger. "Oh, and the night hasn't even started yet."

Someone still needed to explain exactly what was happening. So Carrie leaned forward, and our attention swung back to her. "See, okay, here's what's going on," she said, shifting forward, adjusting herself on the couch so she would be in prime storytelling position. "There is a verse in the Bible—at least, I'm told there is a verse in the Bible—that says all of Christ's followers must also follow the laws that the government sets in their lands. And because the drinking age is twenty-one, it would be a crime if some of you were allowed to drink inside this house."

Carrie paused for a second before continuing. "Those guys"— here, she pointed downward—"have asked that we cancel the party and send everyone home."

Then she tossed up her palms, as if to say, *Yup, this is what I'm dealing with.*

We looked around at each other, our eyes big. Eventually we all turned our attention to Sammy, who had been the team captain that season, and who was also the oldest among us. "Don't look to me for this one," she said. "Tonight, I'm Switzerland." She said she would have had no problem hosting a house party, but she wasn't someone who trampled on other people's beliefs, even if she herself did not abide by them.

We left less than an hour later, bored of sitting around watching people not talk. But when I eventually teamed up with the "downstairs crew" of Sasha, Lisa, and Kelly, I adopted their philosophy of following the laws of the land, even the inconsequential ones like jaywalking. Jesus did not approve of scofflaws, even though he seemed to be one himself, in his own way. I was often told that in God's eyes, all lawbreakers and sinners were the same, regardless of the magnitude of their infractions. Lisa once offered this analogy: *Every sin is a drop of blood into water, corrupting the whole.* And yet I've noticed that fundamentalist Christians seem to respond much more aggressively to gays than to jaywalkers, despite both being, you know, "a drop of blood into water."

Taking the Ambien was like lots of jaywalking, and once I woke up, I waded through a cloud of guilt. We had a game that night against Oklahoma, and I slogged through the morning shootaround, thankful I had a full day to snap out of my drug-induced haze. As our bus pulled up in front of the hotel afterward, Kristen announced she would be taking a walk over to the Grassy Knoll before our pregame meal. If anyone wanted to join, she said, she would be in the lobby in an hour. My teammates looked at each other quizzically, some of them whispering—*Grassy Knoll, what's she talking about?*—as if Kristen had invited them to a picnic on uneven ground. They all shrugged and filed off the bus, ready to tuck themselves back into bed.

I met Kristen in the lobby an hour later, and she asked me if I thought we should wait in case anyone else showed up. I said I didn't think that would be happening. "My teammates aren't exactly history buffs," I said, not even realizing the pun until Kristen laughed and asked, "Pun intended?" We pushed through the doors of the hotel and walked across the street to the trolley. Most of our players grew up on the West Coast or in the heartland, where John F. Kennedy was just an assassinated president, not a beacon of hope for a whole generation, as he was for many New Englanders. My mom, having grown up Catholic and Irish in Rhode Island, adored JFK, and so I did, too. Unfortunately, the Sixth Floor Museum at Dealey Plaza, just up the street from the Grassy Knoll, happened to be closed that afternoon. Kristen and I cupped our hands to the glass and peered inside, trying to get a peek at what we would have seen, but it was unsatisfying.

The afternoon was warm and muggy, the sun dodging in and out of clouds. We walked down the street and stood on the sidewalk in front of the Grassy Knoll, staring out at the paved blacktop on which JFK's topless black limo had once traveled. There was a small white "X" on the road, commemorating the spot where he was shot. I tilted my head up toward the clouds and squinted at the sun trying to burn through. Then I glanced down at that white X. I wanted to walk into the road to inspect it—was it tape? was it paint?—but cars kept zooming past, picking up speed as they approached the on-ramp for the highway. I superimposed people onto the Grassy Knoll and tried to recreate the infamous scene in my mind. I wanted to feel the moment, to become a part of the few seconds that had so dramatically changed the course of history. It wasn't so much about JFK for me, but about connecting with the passage of time itself, which has a way of reminding us that the wide berth of the past and the endlessness of the future are constantly swallowing the drama of our present. And yet truly feeling anything that March afternoon proved impossible, like trying to reach for the string of a balloon that had already floated out of reach. I watched it drift away, the scene in my mind, and when I turned back to the road, all of it was just another city block.

I looked at Kristen, my heart still heavy in my chest, and asked if she was ready to go.

"Bummer it was closed," she said, already heading toward the trolley.

CHAPTER 14

(Don't) Stay the Night

I heard from Cass just once while I was in Dallas. It was the night we were eliminated from the Big 12 tourney, which happened to be the same day Kristen and I visited the Grassy Knoll. After losing to Oklahoma, we returned to our hotel and I went straight to my room to check my phone. I hadn't brought it with me because I told myself, *Out of sight, out of mind.* I also told myself, *I'm better than this.* Of course, I wasn't. I ruminated about that lonely little phone, sitting on my bedside table, and I clawed my way back to it as quickly as I could, chastising myself for not bringing it with me in the first place. I pictured it bursting with messages from Cass, who would have a believable explanation for her silence, the words like aloe to my burnt heart.

But there was only one message from Cass, and the contents of it made me wish there had been no message at all. "Sorry about the loss," she had written. "Safe trip back." I read the text a few times, trying to pull meaning from it, finally realizing there was none—at least not the kind I wanted. And, even worse, I was sure there would be no more messages. I glared at my phone, as if it had transmitted the wrong text, as if the problem existed inside the device itself.

Dee came through the door a minute later. "Dang, you're in a hurry," she said. "Can't even hold the elevator for me?"

I pretended not to hear her.

—⁊⁊⁊—

We returned to Boulder late the next afternoon. I lugged my bags to my room and shut the door, collapsing onto my bed. The sun was still bright, and the flimsy blinds that covered my window were worthless. I closed my eyes and draped my forearm across my face. I let myself drift off for a minute and considered crawling under the covers and going to sleep. My limbs felt heavy, as if moving them would be a cumbersome process. I thought about Cass. I wanted to reach for my phone, which was buried somewhere inside my backpack, but told myself not to do it. Checking the phone had become an addiction, a drug. I battled the urge for a minute, then succumbed, rolling over and sticking my hand into my bag, rummaging around until my fingers found the buried treasure. I didn't look at the screen, not yet. I placed the phone on my chest and waited. This was the best part, when I remained hopeful: a peak, then a valley.

I closed my eyes again and recalled that evening pumping gas in the rain. I thought of the message Cass sent: *Nothing worth having comes easily*. I repeated the phrase in my mind, over and over, rearranging the words to make jumbled Yoda-like sentences: *Easily, nothing worth having comes . . . Worth having easily, nothing comes*. Eventually, the real phrase flashed back into my mind, bold and big, like a banner hanging across my room.

I opened my eyes and sat up. I walked over to my Toshiba laptop computer (which now appears in my mind like a boxy relic) and logged into my student email. I typed Derek's address, and "I'm so sorry" as the subject. Then I moved the cursor over the body of the email and offered him the most simple, direct words I could think to say: "I just can't do this anymore. It's not what I want. I'm sorry." Before I could really think through the finality of the moment, I clicked "send" and watched the icon of a paper airplane zoom into cyberspace. By that time, Derek and I were rarely speaking, so I imagined my note wouldn't come as a shock, but I still surprised myself with the callousness of the action. I mourned our relationship for a few seconds, glancing at the framed picture of him I kept on my desk. Then I closed the lid of the laptop, feeling like I was closing the door on him, too. (The two of us would talk more in the coming days, his calls persistent, but I never changed my mind about ending it. I just tried to give him as much closure as I could, which was very little because I wasn't yet willing to tell him the real reason it was over.)

I emptied the contents of my backpack, tossing a stack of books onto the bed and filling the empty space with an outfit for the next day. I fished my toothbrush and toothpaste out of my overnight bag from Dallas and transferred them to the backpack. I slung it over my shoulder and took a quick look around my room to make sure I wasn't forgetting anything. But there was really nothing of value to forget, because at that moment I was carrying everything I needed in my heart.

Dee was in the kitchen as I passed through, pouring a tall glass of orange juice. "Want to read some verses with me tonight?" she asked.

"Maybe later," I said, walking out the door before she could ask where I was going. On the way to my car, I wondered if I was making a decision that would pave an entirely different future, as if I had come to a fork in the road and at the very last second swerved in a direction I hadn't expected to travel, spinning the wheel and sweeping across the lanes, heading for an unfamiliar exit. I held tight to the straps of my backpack and put one foot in front of the other until I was sitting in my car and turning on the engine.

As I drove, the sun was low on the horizon, dipping behind the Flatirons and illuminating them from behind. My backpack was resting in the seat next to me, a passenger facing forward, ready for whatever the future held. I had turned off the radio, so when I signaled a turn, the sound of the blinker bounced around the car like a hidden clock. I felt sick with anticipation. I wanted to get there as fast as I could, so I could stop worrying that the place would be empty, that my hope and excitement were a mirage. I glanced at my backpack every two minutes, a visual reminder that, yes, I was doing this.

I parked along the curb and turned off the engine. The light on the left side of the house was on. I could still drive away, and I thought about doing so, letting my hand linger on the key for a second. But there are moments in life when walking away is more soul crushing than failing, and at some point over the past twenty minutes, I had decided that this was one of them. I yanked the backpack off the seat and walked to the front door—her front door. Excited, nervous, still needing plenty of guidance, I knocked as if my future stood on the other side. Cass appeared a moment later, pulling the door inward. Her eyes dropped for a quick second, down to her feet, and when she looked at me again, her smile was lopsided, like she couldn't fully commit to the emotion.

"Can I come in?" I asked, because I didn't know what else to say.

She took a small step backward, leaving just enough space for me to squeeze inside. I sucked in my breath and slipped through the opening. I felt like I had arrived at a shop a moment before closing time and that the proprietor wished she had locked up just a little bit earlier. I stood in the mouth of the narrow hallway, the one that led to the small room Cass rented on the left side of the one-story home. I was still holding tight to the straps of my backpack.

"What's that for?" Cass said, pointing vaguely in the direction of her own back, where a bag might have been.

"This?" I put my thumbs under the shoulder straps and lifted the weight for a split second, then let it drop. "Well, it's kind of a long story . . ." I smiled, still thinking I could chip away at the wall Cass had built, although I had no clue what I would do if I accomplished that.

Cass crossed her arms, raised her eyebrows.

"It's just that . . ." I began, taking a deep breath. "We got back from Dallas, and I was lying in my room thinking, and I remembered what you said a few weeks ago. You remember? The part about nothing worth having comes easily?" I patted the pocket of my jeans, where my cell phone was stashed, because for me that's where those words existed. "So I'm thinking about what that means, and I wanted to see you. You had said—and I know this was a while ago—that I could stay the night sometime, just pack a bag and go to class from here."

I looked at Cass. Her eyes were softer now. I lifted my shoulders to my ears and turned my palms up, as if showing her I wasn't hiding anything. "So that's what I did," I added, letting myself go slack afterward, open and vulnerable, willing to be her puppet if that's what she wanted.

She smiled, genuinely now, soft and bright and full. "Oh, Kate," she said, shaking her head. "You're just not ready. I'm not sure you know yet what you really want, and I promised myself a long time ago that I wouldn't get wrapped up in someone else's coming-out process—because it's hard and draining and painful."

She stepped toward me and opened her arms. I had never hugged Cass before, had offered nothing of myself except words and time, too scared even of letting my hand linger on the gear shift, lest our hands should touch. But I stepped into her hug.

"You should go back to your apartment," she whispered into my ear. "Anything between us would end badly because we're in such different places in our lives."

She let go, then practically spun my shoulders around, like I was a kid heading to school for the first time, needing encouragement. She seemed to point me toward the door, a hand on the small of my back. I crossed out through the threshold I had just entered. Cass waved and closed the door gently behind me, so I could barely hear the click of the lock catching. The sun had disappeared behind the Flatirons and the darkness of night was settling over Boulder. How long had I been inside the house? No more than five minutes. I did not pause upon hearing the door close behind me. On legs of rubber, I walked directly to my car and started the engine. I did not cry, but I noticed how much it hurt to swallow.

A few minutes later, I wrapped myself under the covers in the same position I had been not even an hour before. When I startled awake during the night, I tried to convince myself that I had never made the trip to see Cass, but by morning a new cloud of melancholy had descended over me, and trying to convince myself it didn't exist would have been like disputing gravity. I felt like everything inside of me was pressing against something it shouldn't be, as if someone had removed my skeleton.

I was a crumpled mess.

CHAPTER 15

Holy Shit . . . I'm Definitely Gay

The ball was in the air for the opening tip, and that's what I was thinking.

Holy shit . . . I'm definitely gay.

As in gay gay.

This wasn't just a one-time thing, an anomaly, a girl crush. I wasn't just in love with Cass. Or distracted by starting a new friendship. Or confused. Or experimenting (which is hard to do when you haven't even kissed a girl). And I wasn't being tempted by the devil, as Dee had hypothesized the night before the game. "This is exactly what Lisa said would happen, remember?" Dee announced as we drove home from practice. "She said the devil would try to steal you from Jesus—and you know how the devil is."

I did? I wanted to tell Dee that, no, I did not know how the devil was. And furthermore, what I had been feeling and experiencing the previous few weeks was more real to me than any Bible verse or prayer session had ever felt. Instead, I simply said, "Hmmmm," making my voice sound half-hearted, like a loud exhale, as I stared out the window.

A second later, Dee concluded, "The devil will use any means necessary."

I thought to myself, *If the devil uses love to win souls, what makes him any different than God?*

But I knew these feelings weren't from the devil, because in the moments when I was most honest with myself, I understood that I had felt this way all along; I just didn't have the vocabulary and framework to give my feelings context. I wasn't "going through a phase," as my mother and father would later suggest.

I . . . was . . . gay.

—⁂—

As my self-realization buzzed inside my brain, the word "gay" ricocheting around, the ball was tapped into the backcourt, near where I was standing. Instinctively, I darted to corral it, and the rest of my team ran downcourt toward our hoop. I dribbled a few times, then passed the ball to the wing, starting us in our offense. On one of the next possessions, I took an open shot from the outside. I missed, but the ball felt good coming off my hand, better than it had in weeks. I made my next shot, a three-pointer, and my next shot after that, also a three. After my third three of the half, I found myself picturing Cass in the stands, even though I knew she wasn't there. I hoped she was watching on TV, and that maybe my performance would convince her to reconsider me—to reconsider the possibility of us.

We were leading North Carolina at halftime, and as we jogged into the locker room, Kris gave me a high five and an encouraging slap on the back. "That's just what we needed!" she yelled. Before the start of the second half, I looked again into the upper corner of the arena but saw only a few patches of empty seats, the bright lights reflecting off the silver benches. I took a big gulp of Gatorade from a small paper cup and told myself I wasn't disappointed, which was as pointless as telling yourself it doesn't hurt when you slam your shin into a coffee table. Because it does, and you just have to wait for the pain to pass. My eyes dropped to the fans just behind the bench, and I saw my mom and dad, wearing their Colorado Buffaloes gear. They were chatting happily with another couple, the parents of a teammate. I crushed the empty paper cup in my hand and dropped it into the garbage next to the bench. Coach Barry, head high, shoulders back, strode past me and said, "Keep it up."

I did. We did. We won by 20 points, advancing to the Sweet 16 of the NCAA tournament. I had scored 16 points, more than my season average, and now we would travel to Knoxville, Tennessee, to keep playing, to try and advance to the Final Four in San Antonio.

"Now that was a team victory," Coach Barry said in the team room after the game, pacing in front of us as we sat like students. (We held all of our meetings, and watched film, inside the team room. The adjacent locker room was seen as the players' space, where we turned up our music and the coaches rarely ventured.) "That's how you play basketball," Coach continued, pausing to make eye contact with each and every one of us. "Now let's keep this thing going. If we play like we did tonight, I'm not sure anyone can beat us."

We jumped out of our seats and everyone extended a hand into the middle. We were still dripping sweat, exuding excitement. "'Buffs are one,' on three," Coach Barry said. "One . . . two . . . three . . ."

"Buffs are one!" we shouted in unison, the same words we said at the beginning and end of every practice, before and after each game, win or lose. We all filed out of the team room, except for Kyra, who had scored 30 points and now had media obligations with Coach Barry. Some of my teammates turned to the right, heading for the locker room. But I had made a habit of going back out to the court, where friends and family waited, before I showered.

"You going out there now?" Dee asked, tossing a thumb in the direction of the floor. I nodded, and she said, "I shall join you," pivoting on the heel of her sneaker and matching my steps. The hallway was narrow, the walls white, all of the color coming from framed pictures of former players and blow-up photos of action shots from important games in CU history. My right arm was extended to the side as I walked, my fingers trailing behind me, brushing the wall of memories.

"You were awesome tonight!" Dee said, throwing her arm around my shoulders. "Can you believe we're in the Sweet 16?"

I wrapped my left arm around her waist and gave her a squeeze. "We beat North Carolina!" I said. "Did you see them on the sideline before the second half, trying to put on those breathe-right strips?"

Dee started laughing. "Yeah, I was like, 'Breathe-wrong baby!' And the adhesive wouldn't stay on because of the sweat," she said happily. "I think the altitude scared them. They were huffing and puffing."

"They were so gassed," I added, as we walked through the mouth of the tunnel that opened up to the arena floor. "I think they convinced themselves there was even less oxygen than there actually is."

Dee waved to her father and brother, who were seated in the family section. She turned and enveloped me in a hug. "Sweet 16!" she repeated, but I got the sense she had wanted to say something else. I thumped her on the back before letting go. "I love you lots," I said, because adding the "lots" seemed to soften the sentiment, taking away some of the intimacy. I didn't want to make her feel awkward.

"Awww," she said, pulling back and looking at me, then adding, "Ditto, Kater Tot," which was pretty much the most Dee thing to say, ever. I shook my head as she walked away, amazed at how distant that shared moment had felt, each of us hedging our bets, not wanting to make ourselves vulnerable.

My parents were leaning against the railing of the stands, my father towering over my mother. "Mommy!" I said, playfully, giving her a hug before turning to my dad. "Dadio!" I leaned into him, resting my head on his chest for a second.

"What a game!" my mom said, her eyes shining. "You were so good." She paused before adding, "And so was the rest of the team, of course," with a wave of the hand and a sly grin.

"Your shot came back just in time," my dad said. "Have you been in the gym shooting extra?"

Oh, if only it had been that easy. If only it had been as simple as faulty mechanics—something I could have worked out during a few late-night hours of shooting, like tinkering on a car—instead of the complexity of a human problem, when the mind refuses to work in harmony with the body.

"Just in the nick of time," I said, snapping my fingers, adding a visual to the nick-of-time-ness with which my shooting had returned.

"Where should we go to celebrate?" my dad asked. "Chili's?"

CHAPTER 16

"To the Mets!"

Dee's college career was over, and she was drunk. Like, really, really drunk. Like, so drunk that if she ran into Jesus, she would probably give him a high five and thank him, words slurred, for dying for her sins. Actually, more than that: dying for everyone's sins.

Ohmygodthankyousooooomuch Jesus . . .

We had lost to Villanova in the Sweet 16, a heartbreaker of a game in which we were ahead going into the last couple of minutes, then couldn't make a basket on our final few possessions. I missed an important shot that might have changed the outcome, but wouldn't necessarily have done so—or at least that's what I told myself. After our charter bus pulled into the Coors Events Center, we had our end-of-year meeting, then cleaned out our lockers. It was early afternoon on a Saturday, and the sun was shining, a hint of warmth in the early spring air. A few of us walked out together afterward and paused in the parking lot, huddling near our cars.

"So . . . we're hosting a party tonight," said one of the younger players. "Everyone's welcome to come, or not come, whatever—no judgment either way." She looked at Dee and me when she said this last bit, knowing how much time we spent at Bible study, and how unlikely it was that we wanted to ingest large amounts of liquor.

"Thanks for the invite," Dee said, cheerful, but non-committal.

A few hours later, in the living room in the middle of that house party, Dee was pretending she was the Statue of Liberty, challenging anyone passing by to try to push her off-balance. "Go ahead—try to push me over," she said repeatedly, believing herself to be ram-rod straight, when in reality she was constantly toppling over, as if a crosswind kept whipping through the living room. She was unable to stand up straight—"majestic" was how she put it—and her invisible torch, a beacon for all those wretched masses, was constantly sagging. I have no clue who or what encouraged her to become the Statue of Liberty that night; I only remember how terribly bad at it she was.

I don't remember these specific details because I, too, had been drinking.

—⁂—

I assumed we weren't going to the party. I unpacked my bag, taking the extra toiletries that had been sitting on the shelf inside my locker—deodorant, lotion, perfume—and stacking them on my desk. I was considering going to a movie when I thought I heard Dee call my name. I opened the door to my room and waited.

"Kate, come here!" she yelled again, and I left my bag, now half-emptied, and joined Dee in the living room. She was lounging in the recliner that faced the TV, although the TV was off. Out of the corner of my eye, I saw something on the circular kitchen table. I glanced over to find a frosted silver bottle and two small shot glasses atop the plastic red tablecloth.

"What's this?" I asked, inspecting the label on the bottle, written in Russian. Obviously I knew what it was, but I couldn't really understand how it had ended up on our kitchen table. It seemed as out of place there as a penguin on our couch.

"It's vodka," Dee replied, still facing forward.

If I had been in arm's reach, I would have gently slapped her on the back of the head. Instead, I rolled my eyes, for my benefit only, and said, "Yes, thank you for pointing that out. What I meant by that question was, why is this here and how did we get it?"

She stood and took the bottle from my hands. "I found it in the back of the freezer," she said. "Who knows how long it's been there, but I don't think vodka goes bad. I think it's already aged or something. And, really, how would we know if it tasted bad? It tastes bad already."

The bottle was opened, but it looked like only a little bit of the alcohol had been poured. Dee brought the bottle to eye level to gauge how much was left, then she lifted a shot glass. Slowly, like someone who had never done it before, she filled the glass with vodka. She did this twice, lowering the second shot glass to the table, so it could rest next to the first. Then she lifted the bottle again to eye level, to see how much we had used.

"I don't understand what's happening," I said.

"Jesus turned water into wine, didn't he?" Dee said, placing the bottle back on the table, taking care to put it on the ring of condensation that already existed.

"Indeed, he did," I answered, looking over at the recliner to see if she had been reading her Bible, but it was nowhere in sight.

"So, I don't think Jesus is against drinking," she said. "If he was, why would he turn water into wine? That wouldn't make any sense."

I didn't really feel like much of an authority about what Jesus was or wasn't against, so I said nothing, hoping Dee didn't need my help to reach whatever conclusion she was clearly already on her way to reaching.

"I think maybe Jesus knows that life is hard," Dee said, nodding as if she had just stumbled upon a nugget of wisdom. "And he has given us certain things to make it easier."

I realized then that the Bible can say whatever you want it to say, can mean whatever you want it to mean. There are rules in the Bible for pretty much everything, and there are other rules that free you from following the first set of rules. Everyone comes at the Bible with his or her own hopes and bias. And then that person makes the Bible dance. On that night, Dee wanted the Bible to tell her that drinking was okay. I wasn't going to stop her because I wasn't sure I disagreed, and there were a lot of things I wanted to forget—and I was pretty sure a large amount of vodka would help in that endeavor. Actually, there weren't a lot of things I wanted to forget. There was one person: Cass. Since she had gently turned me away, I had woken up each morning with a hole punched through my heart. By the end of the day, I had learned to work around the gap, like I was taking a detour around a construction site, but I went to bed each night hoping the next morning would be a little less painful.

"Anyway," Dee said, handing me one of the shot glasses, "I think we need to take the edge off, and I think Jesus would understand."

—⁕—

I don't know exactly how much Dee had to drink, but she was steadily tossing back vodka the way we rehydrated with water at basketball practice. The bottle was half-empty (or half-full, depending on your perspective) when we left for the party, and I'd had only two shots. Lindsay drove us. Dee sat next to her in the front seat, fiddling with the radio and aggressively playing the air drums. Lindsay kept staring at me in her rearview mirror, with a look that said, *What the hell is happening?* I was feeling warm inside, and definitely a little buzzed, so I kept glancing away whenever we locked eyes. I didn't have an explanation for what had come over Dee, other than, "She's drunk."

When we walked into the house party, our younger teammates, who had also been drinking, threw up their hands in celebration and yelled, "Whaaaat? Look who it is!" The alcohol must have had them feeling warm and fuzzy, too, because they were generous enough to ignore the hypocrisy of our behavior. (Dee had always invited everyone to our Bible studies; I had done it, too, but with much less persistence, secretly hoping to collect rejections.) Dee stumbled in the door, happy and hugging everyone, with Lindsay beside her, arm out in case Dee needed steadying. Lindsay's body language looked like an apology: *Sorry I brought someone already drunk to the party where we're supposed to get drunk together.* Dee was oblivious. I said hello to everyone and walked out to the backyard, where a few more people were sitting on the deck, sipping a blue concoction from red plastic cups.

My teammate Ashley caught my eye, then quickly looked away, lifting her cup to her lips and taking a gulp. I thought nothing of it and sat in a plastic Adirondack chair, focusing my energy on seeming completely sober, which was a lot of work given that I had more alcohol in my body than at any time since my senior year of high school. My elbow slipped off the armrest, and my eyes darted around to see if anyone had noticed. They were all chatting about our loss to Villanova. "I will never watch that tape, ever," I heard one of them say.

"Kate, can I get you a drink?" someone asked.

Ashley was standing by the sliding screen door, fingers resting on the black handle, waiting for my answer. The conversation suddenly stalled, with everyone seemingly interested in how I might respond.

"Yeah," I said, trying to sound nonchalant. "Sure."

The silence extended an extra beat, and then my teammates started talking again, picking up right where they had left off. The decibel level rose—apparently I had popped the cork on the evening—and a minute later a red plastic cup was being lowered into my line of sight, like an offering from heaven. Then I saw sneakers and realized Ashley was back with my drink, gripping the rim with her fingers like a claw. I wrapped both hands around the sides and thanked her for her service.

"Anything for you," she said, and I thought I saw her bow slightly.

Huh, this is odd, I said to myself as Ashley took another deep gulp of her drink. (I would learn later that everyone was downing Kool-Aid mixed with Everclear, which is essentially rubbing alcohol. Our party "punch" probably could have intoxicated a herd of elephants.) I was wearing a vintage blue t-shirt that had "Mets" written in orange-colored cursive across the front. The tee was old enough that the logo was cracking, the fabric of the shirt worn down to almost nothing in certain places. I know precisely what I was wearing that night because hours later, when the real booze had run out and all we had left was a case of the ambitiously named "Milwaukee's Best," Kyra and I stood over her sink and poured the beer into shot glasses, toasting each one, "To the Mets!" I think she thought it was a funny, meaningless toast, and she might have been mocking my choice of attire, but I remember lifting my shot glass with sincerity, hoping that all of our positive energy might help the Mets have a better season. (It did not.)

Of course, that was near the end of the night, and much would happen before then. First, Dee would have to be brought home and put into bed because she could not stand up on her own. The Statue of Liberty had gone from wobbly to toppled, and it was kind of a downer for everyone walking in the door to see her lying on her side, mumbling and butchering the famous inscription, "Give me your miserable wenches . . . " Ashley volunteered to drive Dee home, on the condition that I come with her. She assured me she hadn't been drinking much; the cup I had seen her with was her first, and she hadn't yet finished it. The two of us lugged Dee to the car, while our teammates scurried over to snap pictures of their fallen comrade. I kept turning Dee away from the flash, like she was a famous celebrity and I was being paid to keep her out of the tabloids. "She would be so upset to see herself this way," I said, as everyone rolled their eyes and told me to get over it. Back at our apartment, we helped Dee into her bed, pulling her sneakers from her heels and making sure none of her body parts were dangling from the mattress. She had a poster on the wall of three puppies—a beagle, a golden retriever, and a lab—and when Ashley and I asked her if she was going to be okay on her own for the rest of the night, she mumbled something incoherent and pointed toward the poster. Ashley and I looked at one another, and then I asked Dee to repeat herself as I leaned in closer.

"Me and the puppies," she said, louder and more slurred than before. "We're gonna party." She reached out her arms like a toddler, and I let her hug me.

"Love you lots, Kater," Dee said, then added, "even if . . ." before flopping back onto the bed and instantly falling asleep without finishing the thought.

I turned to Ashley, who was sitting on the foot of the bed.

"She's gonna party with the puppies?" Ashley asked.

"Apparently that's the plan," I said, standing. "You ready?"

"Will she be okay?"

"She'll be fine," I said. "She's one of the best sleepers I know."

When we returned to the party, Ashley walked directly to her oversized red cup, which she had left on the kitchen counter. I watched her chug it down. She glanced at me on her final swallow and raised her eyebrows. I didn't really know Ashley. She had gone to high school in Colorado, then attended the University of Florida, where she played her freshman season. Apparently she really missed home—mostly, she told everyone, she missed her boyfriend, who attended Colorado State—so she transferred to CU at the beginning of her sophomore season. Per NCAA transfer rules, she had sat out her first year in Boulder; she could practice with our team but not play in games. We spent a lot of time together her first few weeks on campus, and I felt that all-too-familiar pull of attraction. But before it morphed into anything real, Ashley started behaving strangely and acting rudely toward me, so we stopped speaking outside of practice. It had been that way for six months; I had barely said anything more than "Hey" to her since September. Once, during a practice in the middle of the season, she was running a sprint and failed to finish hard, cutting it short before she got to the baseline. I called her on it, as team leaders are supposed to do—keep everyone accountable. "Hey, Ashley, touch the line," I said, and she flashed me a look that cut me in half. On her next sprint, she ran through the baseline, off the court, and up into the stands before turning around. I remember thinking, "What the fuck?" And I made a mental note that Ashley had some inner demons that probably needed addressing.

From the kitchen at the house party, I glanced at her again. She was long like a swan, her face pulled downward from her blue eyes. She always had this fiercely innocent look, but I could never tell if she was protecting her innocence with a veneer of fierceness or whether it was the other way around. That night she was wearing running sneakers and jeans, and a sliver of her midriff showed below her red sweater. I thought I glimpsed a belly button ring. Later, I would find a tattoo on the back of her shoulder, and I would ask her a dozen questions about why she got it. (Ashley has another tattoo now, in honor of me, of us, and I can only imagine that someone else, maybe more than one person, has asked the story behind it. Every once in a while, I find myself wondering how she might explain it.)

Just then, Kyra walked into my line of vision, her dirty blonde hair falling into her eyes, which was very un-Kyra-like because she was meticulous about her appearance. She had taped a sign onto her stomach asking for donations to help pay for the alcohol she had bought for the party. I gave her ten dollars, and she responded, "Much obliged," then kept walking. When she was gone, so too was Ashley, missing from her place across the room. I scanned the house but couldn't find her. As I was turning to walk to the backyard, to pour myself another helping of spiked Kool-Aid, I felt a hand on my shoulder.

"Hey, um . . ." said Camille, pointing to a closed door across the living room. "Ashley asked me to tell you to meet her in there."

"Ashley did?"

"Yeah, Ashley," she said, taking a sip of her beer before adding, "That's all she said. 'Can you tell Kate to come meet me in here.' So here I am, telling you."

"Okay," I answered. "Thank you—I guess?"

My eyes darted between the closed door and the sliding screen leading into the backyard, as I tried to decide what I should do first. Something was telling me I would need a big glass of Kool-Aid to handle whatever was going to happen with Ashley, so I went and poured a drink first, then knocked gently on the door to the bedroom, peeking my head inside. Ashley was sitting on the bed, cradling her red cup in her lap. She took a sip and said, "Come in." I did, slipping through the small space I had made. I left the door slightly ajar because I wanted to keep that connection to the party outside— because I was still just a little bit frightened of Ashley.

"Will you close it all the way?" she asked, and something about the vulnerability in her voice, the softness, made me gently push the door into place. I sat on the wooden floor and leaned against the bed frame, making a conscious decision not to sit next to her on the bed, because that would have been making a statement I wasn't sure I wanted to make. I placed my cup on the floor next to me and extended my legs, crossing them at the ankles. Ashley sighed, seemingly disappointed about where I had chosen to sit, but she began talking right away.

"Do you remember this fall," she said, "and how we would hang out sometimes?" I wasn't sure if this was really a question or if she was just warming up and needed me to be quiet, listen, and let her work through her opening. The pause dragged on, and I realized she was going to need my help.

"Of course, yes," I said. "I remember."

"And then how, all of a sudden, I just started acting like an asshole?"

"Yes, I remember that, too."

"Well, I never told you this," she continued, "because you had a boyfriend and he was going to be a doctor, and everything you did seemed so perfect, the future all in place, and I . . ."

"Wait, what?" I cut her off midsentence and looked up at her. "Nothing about me seems perfect. My life is a fucking mess."

Ashley rolled her eyes. "You're perfect," she said. "You're not the disaster that I am, making all these stupid decisions, like transferring for a boy when I don't even like boys." She watched me for a second to see if those last few words had any impact, if they would trigger something in me.

After a beat, she said, "I know about Cass."

The sound of that name made my heart skip, as if Cass had just walked in the door—as if hearing her name from someone else's lips made her, somehow, mine. I looked away, staring down into my blue liquid and swirling it inside the cup. I didn't care how Ashley knew. (Turns out, the gay community in Boulder was very talkative.)

"I can't tell you how excited I was when I heard that," she continued. "What I mean is, it gave me hope."

My mind was still on Cass, on how badly I wanted her to be the person in this room with me right now. I pressed my eyes closed like a little kid who thinks she can change the scenery if she wishes for it hard enough.

"Hope for what?" I asked, opening my eyes, looking at Ashley looking at me. She scooted off the bed and joined me on the floor, her back against the bed frame, too, her left knee next to my right.

"I thought there was something between us before, earlier," she said. "And it scared me, so I started acting like an asshole. I wanted to make you think that I didn't care about you at all. But the only reason I acted that way is because I did. I mean I do. Care about you."

She paused, then said, "Uh, anyway, I'm not making myself as clear as I want to. I was hoping you'd give me another chance to be your friend, and then maybe we can see where it goes."

I tried to remember how I had felt about Ashley when I first met her. There had been something between us, yes, but then she quickly killed whatever it was, turning into someone I disliked. Now here she was, asking me to forget all of that, to start over, to give her a chance. Ashley would never be Cass, no matter what I told myself, and I told myself a lot of different things.

"Okay," I said. "Let's be friends again."

I was desperate for someone to close the hole in my heart.

CHAPTER 17

Graduation Day

Every time I ran into Ashley, often after classes near the parking lot by Dal Ward, she would reach into her back pocket and produce a folded piece of notebook paper, on which she had written me, in her tiny script, a note that covered front and back. She usually summarized her day, while also sprinkling in compliments and praise, emphasizing how frequently her mind had turned to me. She often wrote in red ink. She was serious about winning my heart, and I was ambivalent about guarding it from her. At first, I didn't think she would be able to keep up the pace, but after a few weeks, I realized she was prepared to do whatever it took. Ashley was one of the most competitive people I had ever met, driven by a deep insecurity that she would never be good enough, each victory just something to distract everyone from how absolutely average she believed herself to be.

It wasn't hard to understand the roots of her behavior. Ashley's mother hid liquor in the cabinets, behind the peanut butter and cereal, then drank alone at night when she thought no one was watching. Ashley's father was raised in a military family, and anything less than his brand of perfection called for dismissal. Ashley thought love was something you earned, like grades, instead of something you could be given freely. She thought that being with me would make her a better person, and she repeatedly wrote that exact sentiment in her notes, as if I possessed a confidence and goodness that would rub off on her like chalk if she could just get close enough. She was busy erecting a pedestal and hoisting me onto it, and I was so weak and vulnerable and empty that I probably wasn't difficult to lift. I started to believe that the way Ashley viewed me was reality. I think a person can make you feel like you're so great, you don't even need God, and if that person tries hard enough, which Ashley certainly did, she can make you do things you never considered.

At first, I let myself confuse flattery for love. The two of us started hanging out a lot that spring. And although I had one year left of eligibility for basketball, I was graduating that May and had an internship set up in New York City, at *Late Night with Conan O'Brien*. This is all to say, I was continuing to put one foot in front of the other. The facade of my life was still intact, even if the framework, the hidden beams holding it up, were splintering.

The weekend before graduation, Ashley and I joined some of our teammates for a game of flag football in the recreation fields on campus. Ashley was sinewy and strong, truly athletic in a way I would never be. My main asset was superior hand-eye coordination and cat-like reflexes. I was like a character out of X-Men: even with my eyes covered in shampoo, I could catch the soap in mid-air if it slipped off its holder. We won the flag football game, and Ashley offered me a ride home. As soon as we settled into her white Saturn, she ejected the CD from the dashboard and handed me the disc.

"I made this for you," she said. "It's a mix. I chose each of the songs for a reason."

"Wow, thank you," I said with a smile. I looked at the silver plastic, which was reflecting the sunlight, and tilted it so I could read what she had written in blue Sharpie on the surface. She had titled the compilation, "To the Mets!" And below that she had drawn a cross, next to which were two people, presumably women, dribbling basketballs.

"Because that's the night all of this started," she offered before I could say anything. "And because you love Jesus and we both play basketball."

I nodded and pushed the CD back into the player. "Let's check it out," I said.

She started the engine and shifted into reverse. The first song was Mario's "Nikes Fresh Out the Box," a little ditty about how Mario likes this one girl so much that he vows to treat her, you know, as good as he treats his Nikes when he first takes them out of the box—which apparently is really, really good, better than he usually treats his women. I looked down at my own sneakers, which were dirty and old, and said aloud, "I need shoes."

We had been backing out of the spot slowly, but Ashley slammed on the brakes so hard that we were both thrown into our seat belts. I looked at her, confused. Her right arm was wrapped around the back of my headrest because she had been negotiating the reverse.

"What did you say?" she asked, her eyes big and hopeful.

I pointed down to my feet. "I just said that I need shoes."

Her arm flopped off the headrest onto the middle console, and her eyes fell, briefly, to the space between us. "I thought you said, 'I need you,'" she admitted. "And my heart nearly exploded, because I need you, too." That was Ashley, putting all her cards on the table in a way I never could.

I laughed, which didn't seem like the right response, so I let it quickly die, then replaced the silence with, "I'm sorry, I didn't mean for it to sound like that. I was just noticing that I need new shoes."

"That's okay," she said, still reversing out of the spot. "You just got my hopes up is all."

"I really didn't mean to," I replied. "But, as a consolation prize, what about if we go to the mall and find me a new pair of shoes?"

As we drove, I kept picturing Ashley's face, open and expressive, filled with excitement. There was something about the way she had said, "I thought you said, 'I need you,'" all fragile and vulnerable, that made me want to say it for real, to wrap my arms around her and try to make her feel loved and wanted.

I would end up spending countless hours inside that white Saturn. The interior was cloth, a dark charcoal. Ashley had replaced the stock CD player with a Sony, and she spent the majority of rides shuffling discs from the sleeve above her visor into the player. "Song ADD," is what she called this practice. We rarely listened to a song in its entirety, instead skipping through a disc in twenty minutes. I asked, on more than one occasion, why we never listened to a whole song. She told me there were too many good songs in the world and that she wanted to hear them all. Every once in a while she would play a song in which I'd lose myself. I'd feel its rhythm and tap my heel in time with the beat, staring out the window, anticipating the next line, the next chorus. I'd forget in those moments about her habit. And when she did skip ahead, as she invariably did, it felt like she had yanked a blanket from my feet and exposed me to the cold. I would snap my eyes from the scene beyond my window—the horizon at dusk, the freshly fallen snow, the highway mile markers— and glare at her. She usually shrugged, that's all, like she couldn't help herself. Sometimes, if she felt playful, she would hold the shrug, pin her right shoulder to her chin, and bat her eyelashes at me, as if to say, *You love me.*

—∞—

My parents flew into Boulder the day before my college graduation. They landed late but called from the hotel to ask if I wanted to meet them for dinner. I was dreading their arrival, because I was no longer the same me. I was becoming someone they didn't know, and I had convinced myself that if they came close enough, they would be able to see the changes, my sexuality like a tattoo I couldn't let them spot.

"I'm so tired," I said into the phone, sounding sleepy and pretending to yawn. "I have to be up early, so how about I just see you in the morning?" My mom asked what I was doing, and I said that I was already in bed, struggling to keep my eyes open. I looked across my room at Ashley, who was lying on my bed and flipping through the channels. She shot me a look as I lied, a grin appearing quickly and disappearing a second later, replaced by a serious look, brow furrowed, as if nothing mattered more than finding something to watch.

"You're sexy when you lie," she said, after I hung up the phone.

"Oh, yeah," I answered sarcastically. "Super sexy, I'm sure." I joined her on the bed, leaning against the wall, and kicked off my sneakers.

—m—

I had forced my parents to attend church with me once, back in the fall, about five months before I met Cass. Dee knew that my mom and dad weren't Believers (capital B!), so we were both concerned about their eternal salvation. During one Bible study, my Jesus crew had encouraged me to invite my parents to church. "Kate," I remember Lisa saying, "not to be dramatic or anything, but if you don't do something, your family will be torn apart for all of eternity."

No biggie.

Problem was, I didn't want to invite my parents to church. The two of them had made their beliefs clear, in many ways, over the years. One time when I was in high school, while we were idling outside a restaurant waiting for my mom to finish using the restroom, my dad lost his brain listening to a radio broadcast in which an athlete thanked God for the victory. "Oh, okay, so now God is a New York Mets fan?" he said, turning around in the car to look at me. "And was God also smiling happily while this guy was knocking up three different women?" I don't think he expected me to answer, but I tossed up my hands anyway, like, you got me on that one! My dad hates hypocrisy, other people's anyway, and religion had more than he could stomach. My mom wasn't quite as turned off by it, but they tended to stand united on philosophical issues.

Also, the church that Sasha had introduced us to wasn't at all like the Catholic church I had occasionally attended in my childhood. If that church back home was like a library, quiet and reflective, this new church was like a rave, with people going bonkers for Jesus. This church, Calvary Bible, labeled itself as "Evangelical Free," which meant the same to me as "Random Words Here." I had no idea what any of it meant. The church was on the outskirts of Boulder, nestled near some open fields, and it resembled a daycare center more than the architecturally significant cathedrals of the East Coast. The service began with contemporary worship songs ("Jesus, Lover of My Soul"), which always struck me as trying too hard, the guitars and scratchy voices a desperate attempt at hipness, at relevancy, distracting the flock from the reality that they were dedicating their lives to an archaic book. *Hey! Over here! It's a cute man in tight jeans and black V-neck tee, crooning about the goodness of God in a stylish, worldly way!*

Usually by the end of the second song, a smattering of worshippers in the first few rows had lifted their hands to the sky, just to be that much closer to God. Their souls were so stirred that they needed to literally reach out for him, closing the distance between themselves and their heavenly father. Some put only one arm in the air, like they were grabbing for a light bulb that needed changing, then slowly waved at the heavens in rhythm with the music. Once, someone supposedly spoke in tongues, although I can't verify this claim because he was speaking a language only he and God could understand, so nobody could really call bullshit. When I went to Calvary, I felt like I was watching a movie in which the audio track didn't quite match the film. I was perpetually a beat behind everybody, clapping a moment late, singing the wrong verse, and I always had this sensation that if I could get something to click, it would all make sense to me the way it seemed to make sense to everyone else in that big wooden room.

My parents joined me just that one fall Sunday. They were freaked out, the way you would imagine salt-of-the-earth New Yorkers would be upon witnessing a holy revival, a gathering of aging hippies, wearing Tevas and socks, calling out to their lord and savior. We went to breakfast afterward, and as we sat down and the waitress handed us our menus, my dad sucked in a big gulp of air and said, "Sooooooooo . . . How about those Giants?"

Then we talked about the Giants.

—m—

Ashley and I were both on my bed, but we weren't touching, which was actually impressive, like we were playing a game of Twister on my full-size mattress. She stopped channel surfing and started watching a replay of "Saturday Night Live" on Comedy Central. I wished she had chosen something else and almost made a move for the remote, but before I could, she flipped the channel until she found ESPN's "SportsCenter," always a safe choice. Cass and I had watched "Saturday Night Live" together a few times during the winter, and they were some of the funniest episodes I had ever seen—probably because everything seemed just a little better when I was with her. I didn't want to start comparing Ashley to Cass by contemplating the relative humor in an episode of SNL, as if Ashley had any control over that.

"This okay?" she asked, gesturing toward the screen with the remote.

"Totally fine," I said.

"What do you want to do?"

"This," I said, leaning my head against the wall. "Exactly this."

Dee and Lindsay had seen me come back to the apartment with Ashley. Dee had been standing in front of the fridge, sipping orange juice directly out of the carton.

"Hey," I had said to Dee, gesturing for Ashley to keep walking.

"Hey," Dee responded, appearing frozen in place, Tropicana carton suspended in midair, like she was a piece of pop art. I could feel her eyes on us as we walked away. Lindsay was in her room, sitting at her desk and listening to music, a bulky pair of headphones covering her ears. She shouted a much-too-loud hello, but never turned around, simply because she wasn't one of those people who gossiped or cared what other people did with their time. Ashley and I slipped into my room, and I immediately closed the door behind us. I felt like my room was the only safe space that existed for us, like it was a friendly embassy in a war-torn country. Who knew what people were saying or doing outside that door?

I had no intention of leaving the room again that night. I just couldn't bear the thought of Dee's eyes on me, her brain churning with thoughts of how I was betraying Jesus. Ashley and I had made it to my safe haven, and now I could pretend that the outside world didn't exist, that what happened within those four walls essentially happened in a vacuum, with no ramifications on my life beyond my bedroom. I did not want to be reminded that this was resoundingly untrue. Ashley scooted closer to me, so our legs were almost touching. I was fixated on the negative space, the millimeter that separated my calf from hers. We watched SportsCenter twice through, with neither of us moving. When the familiar *da-da-DA-da-da-DA* theme started for the third time, and the anchor dove in on the lead highlight yet again, I clicked off the TV so that now the only light was coming from my bedside lamp.

"Oh," Ashley said. "Should I leave?" She leaned forward and reached for her sneakers, unlacing them so she could slip her feet inside.

"Or you could stay," I said. "I mean, why not?" Of course, I could think of many reasons why not. First on the list: I knew that asking Ashley to stay was like opening Pandora's box, that she was passionate and giving but also desperately troubled. I knew if something happened between us, and asking her to stay ensured that something likely would, she'd feel she had a claim to me. At the same time, though, I needed answers about myself. Cass didn't want to take the test with me. Ashley did.

In other words, I did need Ashley.

"I could definitely stay," she said. "If you want me to."

Then she turned her eyes toward me, a strand of her blonde hair like a crescent moon framing her face. She needed me to say it, that I wanted her to stay. And it seemed like such a small request, like she had asked me to pass the salt—the kind of thing you don't refuse.

"I want you to stay," I said easily, because I did.

She put her hand on my knee, using it as an anchor as she stood. A jolt passed through my body, and I realized that was the most we had ever touched. "Can I use the bathroom?" she asked, pointing to the door and frowning because she knew the bathroom was in the hallway, outside of the safe space.

"Of course," I said, even though I didn't want her to leave the room. I didn't want her to run into Dee in the hallway, the two of them doing that dance when you don't know which way the other person is going, and Dee saying something brazenly straightforward, like, "God is disappointed."

"I'll be quick," Ashley said, disappearing through the door. I let my head thud against the wall, not too hard, but just enough to knock myself back into the moment. I blinked, looked around my square little room, taking a mental snapshot. My Bible was on the bedside table, illuminated by the lamp, and I leaned over and grabbed it, putting it atop a pile of books below, in the darkness. For a second, I allowed myself to recognize the significance of the action, but then I heard the doorknob turn and Ashley came into the room. "Mission successful," she said, as I pulled myself back onto the bed and forgot all about how I had just moved my Bible into the shadows.

Ashley had kissed a girl before. She broke up with her boyfriend, or he broke up with her, sometime during the year, and she briefly dated a girl she had played basketball with growing up. I had known this for months, because of an interaction I'd had with Kyra when we crossed paths on campus one cold day. I remember there was dirty snow on the ground from a storm earlier in the week, and also that I was wearing my beanie, the one that looked like a buffalo was thundering across my forehead.

"Oh my God!" Kyra grabbed my arm when she saw me and pulled me close to her, like she was angry and needed to shake some sense into me.

"What is it?" I said, looking at the spot where her fingers were wrapped around my biceps.

"Sorry, sorry," she said, as she let go of my arm. "Get this: Sarah and Jamie are dating." Sarah and Jamie were two of our teammates, and also Kyra's roommates. "Like, they're a couple. As in . . ." Before uttering this last word, she looked around and made her voice very small.

"Lesbians."

Kyra continued: "I guess I should have known! They're always going into Sarah's room and closing the door and not coming out until morning."

Huh.

"Oh, oh, oh!" Now Kyra was shaking her head in disbelief. "Ashley is hooking up with a girl, too. Ah! What is going on with our team?"

"Gross," I said, because this reaction had always served me well, the verbal equivalent of pulling out a piece of glass and deflecting the glare. "That is gross, really gross."

"Totally gross," Kyra agreed.

"I don't even want to picture it," I said, practically spitting out my tongue as if a bug had just crawled into my mouth. Kyra responded by putting her hands over her ears and loudly singing, "*Lalalalalala*," which in retrospect makes no sense at all.

"I, for one, love penis," she said.

"Duh," I answered. "Me, too. So much."

We both started laughing, then high-fived and walked in separate directions.

Now Ashley was in my room, and I was thinking I wanted to kiss her. But I had no idea how to make that happen, as if somehow the whole mechanics of kissing were totally different because she was a girl. I felt like we each had invisible fences around us, and if we leaned in too closely, we would be shocked. The universe, God himself, would literally repel us from one another. I thought how it would be nice just to lay next to each other, no matter what else happened.

"Can I?" Ashley asked, pointing toward the bed.

"Yeah, totally," I said, walking to my closet so I could change into shorts and a t-shirt. I turned my back to Ashley and pulled off my hoodie, then my bra. I tried not to think about her eyes on my naked back, but it was all I could think about. I quickly lifted a shirt over my head, then turned around, facing her. She said nothing, just silently watched me as I laid down next to her. We both turned onto our sides, our hands folded underneath our heads like makeshift pillows. Our eyes were locked, but I kept interrupting the moment by blinking and keeping my eyes closed for a few seconds, pretending I might fall asleep. Somewhere outside the window, a car door slammed.

"What's it like?" I asked, intending to sound cryptic, feeling very much like the only way I could do this was to circle around it, toeing the water, then instantly pulling back and starting again.

"What's what like?"

"You know," I said.

Ashley paused for a moment. "You mean kissing a girl?"

I nodded, slightly, wanting to make it seem like she had introduced this topic, not me. I had never said anything about kissing a girl.

"You could find out," she said, dropping her hand onto the bed, in the space between us, like she was meeting me halfway.

I inched my body closer to hers, a tiny bit, trying to make it seem like I was just getting more comfortable, just rearranging myself. "I wouldn't know how," I said.

"I believe in you," she answered.

I closed my eyes, keeping them shut for a few minutes. I didn't intend to fall asleep, but I could feel my mind shutting down. "Sleepy," I mumbled, and I heard Ashley whisper, "Me too." Then I drifted off.

We couldn't have been asleep long, no more than forty-five minutes, when I snapped myself awake. In my dream, I had been walking across a balance beam; I had started to fall, was leaning too far to the right, when I tried correcting myself, jerking my body. Awake again, I looked at Ashley. Her eyes were still closed, her lips slightly parted, her hand still offered to me in the space between us. From above the bed, the moonlight was spilling in through the blinds. I stirred, inching myself closer to her. There was a dream-like haze to the moment, and being so near to her emboldened me, like anything was possible now that the world was asleep, now that everyone was somewhere else, in their own versions of Neverland.

I moved so that my lips were near Ashley's lips, so near that I could feel her breath as it exited her body. "How's this?" I whispered, and she smiled without opening her eyes.

"You're doing well," she said softly, lifting her hand off the bed and placing it on my side.

I moved even closer, letting my lips linger next to hers, as close as they could get without touching. Then I lifted myself slightly and brought my lips to her ears, whispering, "And now?"

"So close," she said. She still hadn't opened her eyes, but she squeezed my hip tightly, as if to tell me there was nothing in the world she wanted more. I slowly made my way back down to her lips, trying so hard to mask my nerves, to be exactly as cool as Ashley seemed to believe I was. I brushed my lips softly against hers, so softly I might not have done it at all.

"Yes," Ashley whispered, the word one long exhale.

I kissed her again, this time so she knew for sure that I had.

CHAPTER 18

Ground Zero

I left for New York City a week after graduation. I think Ashley thought I might call off my internship and spend the summer with her in Boulder. She made a passive reference about her hope the day before my flight, saying, "Well, you could always stay, right?" We were driving in her Saturn, and the way she said it made me think it wasn't the first time it had crossed her mind.

"Um, no, not happening," I said firmly, without hesitation. "This is the coolest internship ever."

She looked hurt, but I was taken aback that she would even consider having me cancel an internship in New York, at *Late Night with Conan O'Brien* no less, when there were thousands of college students who would mug their own grandmas for the opportunity that awaited me. I had scored the gig by having our director of sports information, an awesome dude named Dave Plati, reach out to an old friend of his, NBC sideline reporter Jim Gray, who then called over to the show offices and asked them to move my resume to the top of the pile. When Dave relayed this story to me, I could actually picture the intern coordinator for Conan O'Brien sitting at her desk, taking Jim Gray's call, then sifting through a stack of paper, finding the one with my name on it, and bringing it to the top. Or at least this is how it would play out in the movie version of my life.

Dee also had an internship in Manhattan, at the NBA league offices in midtown. We were both crashing with my sister, Ryan, who was living in a studio apartment in Battery Park City, overlooking the wreckage of Ground Zero. The unit had been steeply discounted, like a lot of apartments in the area, as part of a government subsidy intended to encourage a return to life-as-normal in Lower Manhattan, after the September 11 terrorist attack on the World Trade Center in 2001. Ryan spent about fifteen hours a day at Goldman Sachs, trading bonds, and when she wasn't there, she was either out with friends or preoccupied at home, monitoring the Asian markets on her Blackberry. So it wasn't like we were going to cramp her style. She had been in the apartment for almost a year and had only unpacked the boxes containing things like cups and towels, the stuff you actually need. What little artwork she owned was still leaning against the walls, and this was back before leaning artwork against walls was cool. All it meant for Ryan was that she was too busy to hang it.

Of course, Dee and I had hatched our summer plan months earlier, when we were still both crazy for Jesus, before I had decided that I was going to kiss girls inside my bedroom late at night, so nobody would ever find out what I was doing. Now everything seemed strained between us, and at one point Dee said she was going to bag her internship and spend the summer in Syracuse with her brother instead, three months of playing Nintendo-64 and eating Cool Ranch Doritos. But nothing between us seemed unfixable at the time; the rift did not feel permanent. We were drifting apart, yes, but I figured the currents would change, eventually pushing us back together. So I convinced Dee to go through with her internship, with our plan to crash on my sister's extra-long sectional from Pottery Barn, by telling her that the two of us could keep up with Bible study. We could hold a little satellite branch in the big city—wouldn't that be cool? I think she latched onto this idea, believing she would use the summer to pull me away from the abyss she thought I was staring into.

Every morning I began my commute to Rockefeller Center by walking along Ground Zero, on the raised, and mostly makeshift, pedestrian walkway that had been erected in the months following the September 11 attack. Although eighteen months had passed since that horrible day, there were still areas of total destruction, just piles of angry twisted metal. You couldn't pass through those walkways and not feel overwhelmed by the sight, by how much work had already been done and how much more was still ahead. I mostly kept my eyes down and listened to the mixes Ashley had made me. Then I would get on the yellow train and ride uptown. (I labeled all the subway lines by their colors, and still do even now that I live in the city.) On my way to the offices of the Conan show, inside 30 Rock, I would stop by the control room, with its wall of TV screens and computers, and log into my email. And every morning, without fail, there would be a long email from Ashley, as reliable as those folded notes she had handed me outside Dal Ward. I was becoming hooked on her brand of all-in. I felt a little rush of excitement each time I saw her AOL address pop into my inbox.

Our first Sunday together in New York, Dee and I walked along the water to Battery Park City, looking out at the Statue of Liberty, which appeared like a toy figurine in the distance; then we sat on a park bench and opened our Bibles. People streamed past us on bikes, roller blades, walking, running, all of them squinting into the bright sun. Dee never claimed to know all the answers, which was probably the only reason I was able to sit with her that afternoon, despite the wall that now existed between us. I still trusted her with my heart, even though it felt like a Ritz cracker, always about to crumble into a thousand little pieces. Yes, she had pulled me out of bed in the middle of the night to tell me that God would never support gay people. She had done that, and yet I never stopped caring about her, never considered her anything but my best friend. Just as she had knocked on my door that night during the winter, she could just as easily knock on my door again and tell me how she'd been all wrong. She was never the kind of person who would stick to what she had said in the past simply because it would look bad to change her mind. I trusted her for the truth. She was, at that time, the only person in my life who heard the truth from my lips the very moment I was ready to speak it.

On that park bench, we looked out on the Hudson River, stared across at New Jersey, and talked about God.

"Who am I to judge, you know?" Dee said, leaning back into the green-painted wooden slabs, pointing a forefinger to her heart. "Who am I to tell someone that they don't know God?"

I nodded. I was still clinging to this idea that I would love God on my terms. Or rather, that God would love me on my terms. Because the terms that most Christians believed God wanted me to follow, that I should live a life without true love, didn't feel like terms at all; they felt like a sentence, a punishment meant for someone evil, not for me.

"That's what I'm saying," I told Dee. "Nobody can know how I feel in my heart. Nobody can know what I believe God is telling me, how all of this feels. That's between me and God, isn't it?"

"What is God telling you?"

I let out a long breath, shook my head, and said, "I keep going back to this idea of love, that it's the best gift God gave us, right? The feeling of loving another human being is powerful and good. It doesn't make any sense to me that God would ask so many people to forfeit that gift. How are they supposed to make it through life?" I paused, then added, "Although, I guess the second best gift he gave the world was wine, so . . ."

Dee laughed, which was the point, but she quickly turned serious again. She closed her Bible and put a hand on the leather cover. "The answers are in here," she said. "Just trust that if you keep going back to the word, you'll find everything you need."

I tried not to let my shoulders slump. Finding answers in the Bible only happened if your heart was bursting with faith, if you believed the Bible's authenticity, so that you simply had to look for the right phrase. But what if you were questioning the truth behind the phrases? How then would you find the answers you needed, if every verse was read with a skeptical eye? My friends always told me, "Faith is believing in what you can't see." Sometimes they used the wind as an example. "You can't see the wind, but you can feel it," they said. "In the same way, you can feel God's presence." I understood the idea, but I also didn't agree that the wind truly goes unseen, because the force of it can move, shake, and sometimes destroy things in our physical world. How can we deny the existence of something that so clearly shows itself to us? When the wind knocks over a tree, and we stand there staring at the roots pulled from the ground like an overturned spider, we all have proof of the wind. Some people believe that God creates the wind, but those who believe that do so on faith, not because they have scientific proof that God does, in fact, control the weather and produce natural disasters to put humans in our place. I know the wind whips because I feel it blowing through my hair; I know gravity is real when I drop my cell phone; I know momentum isn't make-believe when I fly into my seat belt after pressing the brakes. But in the end, when everything is stripped bare, only one thing holds Christianity together: faith. Everything that doesn't have a logical answer requires faith. Except sometimes the thing you can't answer creates a breach bigger than your capacity to believe. And then, like sea water, doubt comes pouring in.

"Can I pray for you?" Dee asked, gently putting a hand on my shoulder. I didn't want her to think I had given up the struggle, so I told her she could. We both closed our eyes, and soon her voice filled the space around us, her hand still resting on my shoulder. "Heavenly Father, we just love you so much," she said. "And we're so thankful for your presence in our lives. God, we come before you today, humbled and broken. And lost. Father, I just want to lift up

Kate to you, that you may give her the strength to battle these demons inside her, to turn away from the darkness that is chasing her."

I opened my eyes and looked out toward the water, my view continually interrupted by the blur of people streaming past. I put my elbows on my knees and cradled my head in my hands. In that moment, I wished I had the power to make life stop, just for a few minutes, long enough to stand and absorb the scene in front of me, to see Dee, head bowed, then walk a few steps away and scream up into the sky. I thought that would be all I needed, just long enough to do that. But I wasn't sure. Maybe I would never press play again.

Right then, I could feel my shoulder being squeezed, and I heard Dee say, "Amen." She opened her eyes gently, as if needing to reacclimate herself with the physical world. "I'm going to keep reading," she said, and I knew she meant keep reading her Bible, and I knew she meant keep reading it alone.

"See you at the apartment," I said, slipping my own Bible into my backpack and lifting the bag onto my shoulder.

"Mmmhmmm," Dee said, not looking up, already immersed in a passage.

I walked slowly along the water, my head tilted up, like I was one of those tourists who seem to have time traveled from the past, or maybe just from Nebraska, mesmerized by what the future has become, stumbling along and staring open-mouthed at the skyline— running into locals who want to get to the goddamn subway, please. I was staying close to the ornate metal rail that separated the cobbled walkway from the water, so I was annoying only the occasional jogger who tried darting inside to squeeze past the crowd. Eventually I hit a corner where I was in nobody's way, and I turned my back to the railing, like a boxer against the ropes. The day was bright and beautiful, with only an occasional breeze that rustled the branches. I watched the wind shake the green leaves, right there in front of my eyes, and I began wondering why God couldn't do something like that, something so concrete that I couldn't deny his existence. I knew what my friends would have said: "But that *was* God! He rustled the leaves for you!" I needed a sign, though, one that could not be confused as a coincidence. I needed a note addressed To Kate, Love God. And rustling leaves, visible to all who could see, would not soothe my pain.

I sank further into the corner, pinned my back against the metal, and asked God one more time to make his wishes for me known. Two women jogged by, talking about dinner plans. A biker rang his bell, speeding up to pass them on the left. A couple of boys were shooting hoops at an outdoor court across the path; the metal net jangled each time the ball touched it. An airplane passed overhead, and I craned my neck to see the speck of it crossing the sky. And that was it. The scene repeated itself, with different joggers and different bikers, like it was all on a loop.

My phone beeped, and I looked at the message on the screen from Ashley: "I miss you." I didn't necessarily think this was a sign either, because she sent some version of that message a dozen times a day. I grabbed the railing and pulled myself fully upright.

"Fuck it," I said under my breath.

—⁂—

I didn't see Dee for the next forty-eight hours. Not until late Tuesday night, when she unlocked the door to Ryan's studio and tentatively stepped inside. I was on the sectional couch, watching TV; Ryan was still at work. Before I could say anything, Dee asked me to join her, saying, "Let's find somewhere quiet to talk, so we won't be interrupted."

We tried the roof, but the door leading to it was locked, so we settled for the dingy stairwell, which we figured would be deserted because we were on the twenty-third floor of an elevator building. The lighting was harsh—bright enough to torture a prisoner by keeping him awake—and the fixtures hummed noisily. I sat on the top step of the flight heading down; Dee sat on the bottom step of the flight heading up. I asked her where she had been, and she told me she had spent much of her time on the roof, praying, searching for God's heart and for answers. She said she had slipped into the apartment both nights and grabbed a few hours of sleep. I said I hadn't heard her, and that I'd been worried about her.

"Don't be," she said. "You're not responsible for me."

I wanted to tell her that we were both responsible for each other, weren't we? But I didn't because I was no longer sure it was true. She looked tired, her eyes hollowed out, her skin dry, and she spoke of the previous two days with an uncommon fatigue, as if she had made her own personal trip into the desert, just like Jesus did, to face and conquer temptation. She seemed to have come out the other side with some sort of conclusion, and now she wanted to share it with me. I waited while she gathered her thoughts, allowing myself a split-second of selfish relief that she still cared about me, even though I could tell that her recent spiritual journey was mostly internal, that she was fighting something.

"Love the sinner, hate the sin," she said finally, after we had been sitting on those cement steps for a while, just listening to each other breathe. It took me a second to piece together the sentence, to understand what it meant, who received the love, what received the hate. Then Dee added, "I think that's how we need to move forward with our friendship."

I slowly repeated the words back to her, like I was learning a foreign phrase and speaking it phonetically. "Love . . . the . . . sinner . . ." I said, as Dee nodded approval. "Hate . . . the . . . sin?"

"Yes," Dee said, pausing to allow me to process. "See, the thing is, I've reached this place where I know how God feels about homosexuality. It's wrong. It's not what he wants for his children. But that doesn't mean, as a Christian, that I can just abandon someone. That's not very Christian-like, either. So what I need to do is make it clear that I don't agree with the sin, with the lifestyle, then go about loving the sinner."

This struck me as very good news. All I needed to do was separate my personal life from the rest of who I was, and I could keep Dee as my best friend. Considering that I didn't even want people to know that I might like girls, that I might be gay, this sounded like the perfect option. A win-win for all involved.

"That's fine," I said quickly. "I totally get that."

I looked down at my sneakers for a second, then back up at Dee, directly into her eyes, and said, "I just don't want to lose everyone in my life. And I especially don't want to lose you."

"You're not going to lose me," she said. "I won't let that happen. Of course, things will probably have to be different going forward. Like even this summer, I just need my space. I probably won't be around much, but if you need me for anything, I promise I'll be there."

I waited.

"And about the apartment stuff for next year . . ." she began, looking down at her hands as if she had scribbled notes onto her palms. Dee and I had already renewed the lease on our apartment for one more year, and we had recruited Lisa to take over the payment on Lindsay's room. The three of us routinely talked about how awesome the year was going to be, how the three of us would praise Jesus together, enjoying the fruits of the life God had bestowed upon us. Dee had a few more art classes to finish before officially graduating; Lisa was taking graduate courses after playing overseas for a year; and I had one year left of college basketball. This plan meant that I wouldn't have to move, that my stuff could stay exactly where it was—a huge relief, since all my other teammates had already made living arrangements for the upcoming school year.

"Yeah? What are you thinking?" I asked, suddenly realizing that maybe Dee had told Lisa what was going on with me. I started tapping my heel, compulsively. "Wait, did you tell Lisa . . . you know?"

Dee shook her head. "That's not for me to do," she answered. "You can tell her what you want, if you want."

"Thanks, okay," I said, feeling excessively grateful to Dee in that moment.

"So, the apartment?" I prodded.

"I've prayed about it, and I think you should stay," Dee said, without looking up from her palms. Her voice didn't hold much conviction. Her decision was like a flag waving in the wind, one that could easily blow the other way any second.

"Are you sure?" I asked, because I wanted to feel more reassured than I did. "Maybe it would be best if I found somewhere else?"

"No, that's not the answer," she said. "And, anyway, as long as what I said before makes sense, I think we'll all be able to figure this out. We're all adults."

"What specific part of what you said before?" I asked.

"Love the sinner, hate the sin," she repeated, and she looked at me finally, her wrists dangling from the edge of her knees as if broken, her eyes clear but tired.

"That's my mindset now," she said.

CHAPTER 19

Love the Sinner, Hate the Sin

Within the first few weeks of living with Dee and Lisa, I realized that I was poisoning myself, that I had essentially agreed to wear a Camelback containing doses of rejection, the release of which was controlled by my two roommates. When Ashley was with me, which was often, I would drive home to the apartment complex holding my breath, my heart hammering, hoping I wouldn't see their cars in the parking lot. I began to view my bedroom, behind a closed door, as my only safe space. I would panic when I walked through the apartment, like I was afraid to find an intruder hiding in the shadows. Even if I returned home before Dee and Lisa, I was unable to concentrate on anything but the sound of cars turning down our road. I felt nauseated each time I heard someone pull into our complex, the engine rumbling, then shutting off. I would listen for footsteps on the walkway to our door, my emotions churning.

Once, believing that the problem was more paranoia than reality, I forced myself, Ashley by my side, to spend the evening hanging out in the living room instead of inside my bedroom. Although I never said what we were doing, I think Ashley knew. We were lying together on the carpet in front of the TV, watching a movie. I think it was the first Harry Potter film, but it's hard to remember for sure because I

was too busy listening to the cars passing outside. Eventually I heard Lisa's car—by that time I could pretty accurately identify her car and Dee's by the sound of the engines—and I fought back the urge to pull Ashley into my bedroom and slam the door. I stayed out in the living room, lying next to her, our eyes glued to the movie as I listened to Lisa's footsteps, her keys jangling. My body tensed as she fiddled with the key, sliding it into the door, turning the lock over. Ashley squeezed my hand once, for good luck, then pulled away.

Lisa stepped inside the apartment and spotted us together on the floor. She froze for a moment, forgetting to shut the door behind her. I saw a shadow cross her face. "Hey," I said, craning my neck backward to make eye contact. I tried to make my voice strong like an arrow, but I think it came out soggy and weak. Lisa snapped back to life. She closed the door behind her and walked past us without looking in our direction, as if we weren't even there. I watched her head down the hallway, and I felt something inside my heart snap and ricochet around my body. A few seconds later, I heard Lisa's door closing, seemingly louder than usual. The sound of it echoed throughout the apartment.

I can still feel that moment, the rejection so simple and true, not messy at all, just a simple black X on my heart.

—〰—

I actually tried to break up with Ashley a week later, but only half-heartedly. Over the summer, I hadn't let myself think about how tricky it might be to date a teammate, especially one as emotional and unpredictable as Ashley. When I returned to Boulder, I allowed myself to believe she would magically morph into a rational and mature person whenever we were around teammates, treating me like just another one of the gang. I quickly learned this wouldn't be the case. On the very first day of workouts, I was shooting with

one of the freshmen when Ashley, seeing us from across the court, marched over to our basket, pinned the ball to her hip, looked at me and then at our teammate, and said, "What the fuck is this about?" I was mortified; the freshman looked impossibly confused, unable to pinpoint what she had done wrong.

One Saturday afternoon during preseason, with our relationship threatening to create even more drama in my life, I asked Ashley to join me for a walk in the meadow behind my apartment. We stopped and settled under a tree. She sat with her back pinned to the trunk, her legs crossed; I sat across from her and began pulling at the blades of grass, ripping them out one by one, creating a small pile in front of me.

"I don't think we should continue seeing each other during the season," I said, proud of myself for this burst of maturity. "Maybe we can pick it back up after basketball ends."

Ashley looked stunned, her face wide open.

"No, you can't do this," she said a minute later, her eyes filled with tears. I could actually see the water rising, like two little sinks overflowing. "We're in love, and we make such a good team," she said, crying so hard that her voice caught as she spoke—that involuntary intake of air that means someone is rounding the corner of upset and speeding toward hysteria.

"Please don't do this," she cried. "You don't want to do this!"

She was right. I didn't really want to break up with her. In that moment, I realized that if she got into her Saturn and drove away, I would be left with Dee and Lisa, forced to fall back into a life that was no longer mine and no longer fit me, delaying my entry into the world that Ashley represented. Also, there was something between us—if I could ever get Cass out of my head. I was also worried that spurning Ashley would create a new kind of drama, which might very well make my life messier than if I stayed with her.

Ashley was shaking her head, slightly but noticeably, as huge dollops of tears spilled from her clear blue eyes, some of them so heavy they missed her cheeks and plopped—I really thought I could

hear them—onto the front of her shirt. She cried the same way she approached most everything in life, with unmatched gusto. I reached my hand to her cheek, pulling the freshest batch of tears from her eyes.

"I'm sorry I said that," I told her. "You're right. We'll figure it out, okay?"

—⁂—

Girlfriend or no girlfriend, I needed to move out. But I needed money to move out, and my scholarship stipend, about eight hundred dollars a month, wasn't enough to cover the rent for my emotionally poisoned apartment plus the deposit and first month's rent on the second apartment I actually wanted to live in, a one-bedroom about a mile from campus. I never had an actual come-to-Jesus conversation with Dee and Lisa, never explained to them exactly how I felt; I simply told them I was moving out, and I don't remember either of them trying to stop me. Both of them made it clear, however, that they didn't want to live with a stranger, and no one in our circle of friends was looking for a room, so I was resigned to eating this second rent.

Money felt irrelevant. I think I would have mortgaged a significant portion of my future earnings in exchange for five hundred square feet of judgment-free space. I might have even paid someone to tell me they loved me and accepted me, fully, no matter what. Perhaps my parents would have been those people, and done it for free, if I had let them see the real me. But I didn't. What I did was hit them up for money—and I lied to get it. I wish I could say this was a one-time occurrence, that I panicked and let some half-truth stand for fact, but the reality is that this was the beginning of a thousand lies, some small and some large, all told in an effort to hide myself. When my mother and father asked me why I needed to move out, I told them it was hard living with two people who weren't on the team anymore, that I felt a disconnect from basketball, that Dee's and Lisa's religious beliefs were starting to run counter to my own, and I was becoming disillusioned with their brand of Christianity. This last part was particularly manipulative because I knew my parents were freaked out about my exploration of religion, telling each other it was "just a phase" I was going through. I preyed on that knowledge, well aware that they would leap at the chance to help separate me from what they considered cult-like, brainwashed behavior. Of course, in talking with my parents, I conveniently omitted any mention of my relationship with Ashley or my ongoing struggle with my sexual identity.

"Check is in the mail," my dad said after I pitched them on why I needed the money. I wanted to breathe a deep sigh of relief, but I noticed that the air still caught in my throat, as if being filtered through a maze. A few days later, I moved out of one apartment and into another. Weeks would pass and I wouldn't see or talk to Dee. Once, I ran into her at the student union and she acted like she didn't know me. She might as well have been encased in glass. "Hi," she said as we approached one another. She stopped for a minute to chit-chat at me about stupid things like the weather and new movies, and I stood there thinking, *So this is what we are now? We're those people?* I couldn't get away from her fast enough.

Then one night during the season, a night that Ashley and I happened to be staying in her apartment, Dee appeared at the door and asked if she could come in. Something about her demeanor seemed stiff, like she was there on official business. She came into the living room and made small talk before turning to me and asking if she could borrow Ashley for a little while. I looked at Ashley, who simply shrugged, like, *Okay—whatever.*

"Sure, yeah," I said, disappointed that Dee wasn't there to see me.

Dee popped off the couch, and Ashley motioned toward her bedroom, where they could talk in private. As I watched them disappear, I noticed that Dee's Bible was tucked under her arm. A swell of rejection washed over me, leaving me feeling damp.

I pulled one of the couch pillows to my chest and hugged it tight. Then I waited. And waited. I stared at the closed bedroom door, even walking over to it at one point and leaning my ear as close as I dared, listening while holding my breath. I heard Dee say, "Well, the Bible says . . ." But then the central heating kicked back on and made it impossible to hear anything else. I shuffled back to the couch and returned to clutching my pillow.

They were in there about an hour. Finally, the door opened and the two of them walked out, everything seemingly normal. We said goodbye to Dee at the front door and waved as she drove away, like she was a relative who had come to dinner.

I turned to Ashley and asked, "What was that all about?"

"She was just expressing concern for our relationship," Ashley said, sounding much more levelheaded about it than I felt.

"You guys were in there an hour," I said, trying to strip my voice of anxiety. We were still standing in the doorway, and Ashley turned and walked back to the couch as I trailed her.

"She took me through the readings in the Bible, the verses— you know the ones," she said. Ashley had been raised in a Christian household and had sporadically attended Bible study when she was younger, but she never seemed to endure the same type of inner struggle that was ravaging me. She loved who she loved, and she didn't seem particularly influenced by how that love might be viewed by people like Dee and Lisa. "We prayed a lot, too, that God would reveal himself to us—me and you—and that we would come to see the truth of our actions. It sounds like everyone is doing a lot of praying for us."

I wanted to launch my pillow across the room, fling it violently against the wall, but instead I strangled it, as if an actual beating heart existed inside the fabric.

"You know, I don't know, I just . . ." I stammered, before finally hitting on exactly what I wanted to say.

"What if I don't want to be prayed for?" I growled.

CHAPTER 20

The Tattered Cover

Ashley parked her Saturn in the lot at Flatiron Crossing, a stylish mall in Broomfield designed to blend in with nature, the structure all red rocks and hard edges—and a Victoria's Secret. The two of us were going to see a movie at the AMC Cinema, and my cell phone rang as we walked across the lot. "Momster" flashed on the screen. I looked at Ashley and showed her who was calling, then put my index finger to my lips.

"Hi, Mom!" I said a second later. "What's up?"

Ashley reached for my hand, but I wriggled out of her grasp and glared at her. She rolled her eyes.

"No, not much, just chilling tonight," I told my mother, an obvious lie. "Yeah, at home, low-key night. Getting ready for the big game and all."

I waved Ashley ahead of me, mouthing, "Buy the tickets," and stopped walking. My mom and I chatted for a few more minutes, about absolutely nothing, before she finished up by telling me how excited she and my dad were for the following week—they were flying out for the opening game of the season—and that she loved me.

"Love you too . . . can't wait to see you . . . okay . . . yup . . . bye," I said, flipping the phone closed.

I'm not sure I thought of my communication as lying, because that feels like a choice you make, a deliberate decision to put something in one drawer instead of another. What I was doing didn't feel voluntary. Telling my mother I was going to a movie with Ashley would lead to questions—when had Ashley and I become such good friends?—which would all end up in some form of a half-truth, or straight-out lie, unless I was willing to come out to my parents, to actually say, "I'm gay, and Ashley is my girlfriend." But that wasn't even something I had accepted myself, not entirely. So how can you lie when you aren't even sure who you are? Everything I was saying and doing was meant to buy myself time—another few hours, a day, a couple of months—during which, maybe, I could unravel the tangled mess that my life had become, an impossible ball of holiday lights. I felt like I had thrown a raging house party while my parents were away, and now I was racing to clean up before they opened the front door. There was no way in hell I could pull it off.

So I went to see *Pirates of the Caribbean* instead.

—m—

The first game of my senior season, against Notre Dame, coincided with my twenty-first birthday. My parents flew into Denver and stayed at the La Quinta Inn in Louisville, about a ten-minute drive from my new one-bedroom apartment. As far as they knew, I was unattached, living alone, focused on schoolwork and practice. So they assumed the three of us would go out to dinner the night before the game, just like we had done on numerous occasions, in the before times. It was such a simple request on their part, but even though I didn't actually have anything else to do, I told them I had already made plans. And instead of dinner with Mom and Dad, I met Ashley and her former high school coach at Chili's, spending the entire time riddled with guilt. Afterward, I drove directly back to my apartment, where I had left my parents, feeling like I had committed some kind of crime.

"Well, we're going now," my father said as soon as I walked in the door, his voice dripping with disappointment.

"Hopefully we'll see you tomorrow," my mother chimed in, gathering her purse onto her shoulder.

"Is something the matter?" I asked, knowing full well that something was the matter, and almost wishing they would just come out and say it, instead of taking the passive-aggressive approach. But we were never the kind of family that discussed our anger as it happened. We were much better at letting slights and wrongs marinate until they were thick and heavy on our tongues; then we bitterly spit them out. My parents weren't quite ready to spit out their resentments, but they would be by the end of the weekend. I continued avoiding them because spending time with them felt like lying to their faces. I was sure that if we went to dinner at the Cheesecake Factory, as we had in years past, they would see the wreckage of my insides and pull my pain to the surface, then express their disappointment in my sinful lifestyle. They would add a fresh layer of rejection—*Kate Fagan, this is not who you are*—to my growing pile.

My father had an earlier flight home because of a business engagement. He left Sunday morning from my apartment, and in the moments before he drove back to Denver, the air inside that small living room was painfully tense. I was almost relieved when he turned to me, his hand already on the doorknob, and said, "You made us feel like shit this weekend. You know that? Like we don't even matter to you. Like we're strangers. I've never been so disappointed in your behavior. You're ungrateful and selfish."

There was nothing for me to say that didn't sound embarrassingly lame—nothing except the truth about why I had behaved that way. I was surprised to notice it had risen up from my chest and actually existed in my mouth, the words ready to be formed. Maybe it was self-defense: I wanted to yell something back at him that would make him understand, that would change the narrative of the weekend. *I was a shitty daughter, yes, but not for the reasons you think!* All I could muster, though, was something pointlessly vague. "I don't know what to say except that I'm going through a really difficult time," I answered. It was like I had brought marshmallows to a knife fight—that's how helpless I felt.

My dad shot me a disgusted look, unable to comprehend how a twenty-one-year-old, who was playing college basketball on scholarship, could be "going through a really difficult time," and yet couldn't explain what, exactly, was so difficult.

"Right," he said, waiting to see if I would say anything of substance. A minute later, he left my apartment, still mad, shutting the door a little too aggressively.

I turned to my mother, a dejected look on my face.

"Yeah, sorry, I'm with him on this," she said, then began collecting her things. Even though her flight was still hours away, she seemed desperate to get out of my presence. I walked into the small bedroom and sat on the edge of the mattress. I wished I could slip out of my skin. I tugged at the cuffs of my sweatshirt and balled up my fists inside of the fabric, rubbing my eyes. I thought of what I should do the second my mom disappeared through the revolving door of Denver International Airport: speed back to Baseline Road, wind into the darkness of the mountains, find a place to park, and take a long walk on one of the frozen nature paths until I was shivering with cold. Or maybe just swing by a liquor store, buy a handle of vodka, return to my apartment, and drink alone. I felt like I needed to do something dramatic, to mirror what was happening inside me. Instead, I took a few deep breaths and forced my mind to stop racing, to stop running away. I sat with my heaviness for a few seconds, trying to calm my anxiety. Tears started spilling from my eyes, and I wiped them away the instant they formed, again and again.

I wanted a hug. I needed sympathy, or even some distant cousin of that emotion—pity, tolerance, any form of understanding, however tentative. This thing, my gayness, was not something I had chosen, I told myself in that moment; it was something that had happened to me. It was as much a part of me as my brown eyes or my right-handedness. I could buy myself blue contact lenses, pretend I was straight, put on a show for everyone (and eventually, I would do the equivalent of that), but underneath, my eyes would always be brown.

I wanted to be held. And I wanted my mom back. I wanted her to say, "I love you no matter what," because nobody else had said that yet, and I was starting to believe no one ever would.

"Can we leave now?" she called from the living room. I stood and rifled through the top drawer of my dresser, searching for my Nike beanie, the one that looked like a Buffalo racing across my forehead. I needed it for protection, to give me some way to hide. I found it and pulled it on, covering my ears and tugging it down to just above my eyes.

"Would you mind driving?" I asked, walking into the living room. I offered my mother the keys to my car because I knew I needed all my faculties to figure out how I was going to say the thing I had decided I was going to say.

"Fine, sure," she said hastily, grabbing the keys from my palm and turning away. I followed her out the door, down the stairs, to my car, climbing into the passenger's seat. She had five hours until her flight, which meant we were leaving two hours earlier than necessary. I had no plan. I fussed with the beanie, pulling it down so it almost covered my eyes. If I could have, I would have made it cover my entire face, like a ski mask.

"What's going on?" my mom asked, glancing away from the road for a second and motioning at the beanie.

"I don't know," I said, releasing my grip. "Just thinking."

She made the left turn onto 28th Street, which quickly turned into Highway 36, heading east. She pressed down on the gas, then locked in the cruise control. We were pointed toward Denver. I slid down in my seat, hunching my shoulders, making myself as small as possible. I glued the heels of my hands to my eyes, as if being blinded by some kind of potent gas. I did not have any words, not yet, but I had actions, and I was hoping my actions would convey to my mother that I had something serious to say, and that once I was able to find the words, I would say it.

"Honey, what is it?" She suddenly seemed more worried than annoyed.

I looked at my sneakers, perched on the dashboard, then slowly answered, "I have to tell you something, but I don't know how to say it."

"Okay," she replied, making the word sound open-ended, like an invitation.

"I just want you to still love me," I said, and started to cry. "Please, no matter what, please tell me you'll still love me."

"I think you should tell me what's going on," she said, gripping the steering wheel with both hands. I hoped she was thinking of the worst possible scenarios: that I had been kicked out of school, that I had gotten a DUI, that I was pregnant. But nothing I could imagine felt worse than what I was telling her. Well, except if I had committed some heinous crime, a thought so absurd that I didn't even allow myself to fully process it. I knew what I was about to say would shatter the vision she had for my life—and, in turn, her life.

I don't remember how long it was until I actually spoke. I kept my eyes buried in my hands for a few minutes, wondering exactly how I had landed in this specific moment and whether I would remember these few minutes for the rest of my life, stored in some part of my brain like a movie on a shelf, ready to be pulled out and watched whenever I needed a reminder of how pathetic I could be. Finally, I lowered my hands and crossed my arms against my chest. I dropped my feet from the dashboard onto the floor, needing them planted firmly on something, even if it was the floor of a car going sixty-five miles per hour. Between rapid breaths, I forced the words out as quickly as I could.

"I think I might be gay."

Once I said it, I sunk back down in my seat, tugging the beanie over my eyes again and curling into the fetal position.

My mom's voice was balanced and reasonable as she asked, "Why do you think this?"

"I just do," I said, my hands fluttering up, like the whole thing was a big mystery. "I can't explain why."

"I can't say that I'm shocked," she replied, still keeping an even keel, which probably should have frightened me more than an emotional response, the kind I had expected when I allowed myself to think of this moment. "We had that one strange conversation last year, and you just seem so much different lately. Is this why you didn't spend time with us this weekend?"

"Yes!" I said, glad she had made that connection. "I love you both so much. I never meant to make you feel that way."

"Who were you with instead?" she asked.

"I was with Ashley, mostly."

"Are you two seeing each other?"

I looked at her, afraid again. "Yes," I said. "Kind of."

I was filled with qualifiers, wanting so desperately to soften the truth with "kind of" and "sort of" and "maybe" and "I think" and "for now" and "mostly." It was a short-term solution that would create a long-term problem, but my vision didn't extend any farther than the front-seat of that car. All I cared about was winning over my mother in that exact moment. I was compromising my future for one hug, for a few comforting words.

We were approaching Denver, and my mom asked if I wanted to get brunch. She had read about the Tattered Cover, an old bookstore in Cherry Creek with a restaurant on the top floor. It felt like a strange thing to be doing, but I said, "Okay, yeah, that sounds good," and she turned in that direction. She parked in a garage, and we wandered into the store, both of us dazed, holding doors for each other and climbing stairs until we were standing in front of the hostess. The woman pointed to the counter, claiming those were the only seats she had available. We nodded and lifted ourselves onto the bar stools. I took off my beanie and tied my hair up in a bun. Without the hat,

I felt naked, exposed. I looked at my mom, worried that maybe now she would see me for the first time and be disgusted.

"If I could run a marathon and not be gay, I would do it," I told her, apparently believing at that time in my life that nothing was more strenuous and awful than long-distance running.

She reached over and covered my hand with her own. "I love you," she said, smiling sadly. "We'll figure this out, okay?"

I nodded vigorously, wanting so much to believe her.

—⁂—

The next day, my parents called me while I was at a volleyball match, Colorado vs. Nebraska. I was sitting in the stands with Ashley and a few of my younger teammates when "House NY" flashed on the screen.

"Hello?!" I said, shouting into the phone so I would be heard above the crowd.

"Where are you?" my dad asked, his voice sounding strained.

"I'm at the volleyball match!"

"Can you find somewhere quiet?" my mom said, her tone and words making my heart sink, her very presence on the line signaling that something was awry. My parents never did that thing a lot of other families do, calling at the same time, on the same line, from different phones in the house. It was just not something that appealed to us; we preferred to have our solo time with one another. I was shaken by this severe breach of Fagan protocol. Whatever was about to happen was so intense that the two of them needed each other.

"I'll call you back in five minutes!" I said, wishing I had let their call go to voicemail.

I excused myself from the stands and shook my head at Ashley, as if to say, *Do not ask; please do not ask.* I walked through the tunnel, into the bowels of the arena, making my way to the training room, where it was so quiet you would never know a match was taking place. I went into Kristen's tiny office and sat behind her desk. When I opened my phone, I saw that my hands were shaking. My thumb was poised over the "House NY" button, but I was too scared to press it. Finally, after a long minute, I hit the button and raised the phone to my ear.

"Hi, Kate," my mother said, sounding crushed. "Dad's on the line, too."

My mom spoke first, saying, "We just want to talk about what you and I talked about before my flight. I know both your dad and I have done a lot of thinking, and we have a lot of questions."

"Listen," my dad chimed in. "Before we say anything else, we want you to know how much we love you." He paused just long enough to let my mom echo the sentiment.

"We love you so much," she said. "And that will never change, ever."

Both of them began crying. Then my father continued, "But we're really struggling with a few things . . ."

But.

All I could focus on was that one word: Why was there always a *but*? My parents swore up and down that they would love me no matter what, and yet the *but* sent me sliding down a rabbit hole, appearing in my mind like miles of quicksand before I could get to the love they were promising. There had also been a *but* with Dee, except hers had been the silent kind. In her version, it went "Love the sinner, hate the sin"—the *but* conveniently omitted from the space just after the comma, trying to sneak past me and steal my heart when I wasn't looking.

I draped my elbow over my eyes and leaned back in the chair, knowing that nothing I said would change what was about to happen. I remember exactly five moments from this conversation, in no particular order. I remember putting my feet on Kristen's desk, and every few minutes wondering if I was being rude for doing so. (I never took my feet down; I just let the soles of my shoes press into the edge of her desk as I held the phone to my ear and listened.)

I remember my father calling me a liar and my mother saying I had lost their trust. Or maybe it was the other way around, with my mother calling me a liar and my father talking about trust. It doesn't matter. In that moment, they were one person. They had called me on the same line; they were united. I remember feeling blindsided and incredulous when my dad asked if I was going to quit the team. "What? Why would I do that?" I said, to which he responded, "So you can deal with all of this," his tone even and steady. I remember my mom asking me how long I had felt this way, and then answering her candidly, which I would quickly stop doing. "Since the end of middle school, I think, or maybe the first year of high school," I said. "But back then I didn't know what those feelings meant." I remember believing, after we had spoken for a long time, possibly an hour, that we would be okay, because my parents had promised many of the things I craved, namely love and acceptance no matter what.

I would soon begin to realize, however, especially when in their presence, that everything was on a slow boil, the unconditional acceptance always feeling just out of reach, my parents seemingly clinging to the belief that something about me would change. Later that year, my mom would send an email to Ashley, telling her that someday we would find men we wanted to marry, and that we would regret this phase of our lives. Ashley and I were in a computer lab together on campus, and she called me over so I could read the note. Our relationship was reaching its conclusion, and Ashley, desperate for it not to end, had been sending my mother emails behind my back, long messages professing her undying love for me. Now my mother had reached her breaking point. She urged us to consider the future: How would we feel when we tried to explain to our husbands that we had once carried on a relationship with a woman?

The trust was broken on both sides, and it would take us years to repair it.

CHAPTER 21

Inside the (Broom) Closet

Practice had ended, but I did not want to leave the court. Most of my teammates had made a beeline for the locker room, to shower and get out of the gym as quickly as possible, but I felt like I needed something, although I wasn't sure what it was. I had untucked my mesh practice jersey, which I did each day as soon as practice was over, signaling to my brain that I was no longer on the clock, the equivalent of loosening a tie. I wandered around the court, dribbling the basketball. Two of my teammates were doing some extra shooting, and I waited them out because I wanted the gym all to myself. For a while, I just sat on the sidelines and cradled the ball to my stomach, resting my chin on the leather, like it was my pregnant belly. Finally, my teammates finished and walked off the court, laughing about something. "All yours," one of them said as they passed.

At first, I didn't rise from my seat. I just looked out at the empty court, around the vacant stands, up at the dark scoreboard. I heard a sound and noticed the building's maintenance director, Karl, pushing a gray garbage can on the concourse, the rhythmic turning of the wheels echoing throughout the space. Eventually I stood and walked to the scorer's table at center court, lifting myself onto the black pad that covered the wood. My legs dangled. I pinned the ball to my right side and rested my open hand on top of it. I sat there like that for a long time, swinging my feet, letting the heels of my sneakers thud against the plastic front of the scorer's table, hitting the space between the two words—"Colorado Buffaloes"— that stretched nearly from one foul line to the other.

Nobody knew me anymore, not really. Ashley thought I was perfect, some ideal human being, which was nice in its own way but also like being airbrushed out of the real world. My best friends were strangers now. I think I would have been okay with losing most of them if I had kept Dee, but I hadn't been able to do that, and I missed her every single day. I thought of my parents, who at that point seemed to have decided, with some help from me, that they only wanted to know certain parts of me, the person who played basketball and attended classes, the parts of me that were easy to talk about at a family party. I was a successful kid, so why fuck that all up with the gay thing, especially when it was probably just a phase?

I swung my legs onto the scorer's table and lay down, perching my head on the ball. I stared into the overhead lights for a few seconds.

"Kate?"

I quickly sat up, returning to my previous position, and searched for the person who had called my name. I saw a silhouette of someone standing in the tunnel; the outline looked like Coach Barry.

"Hi, Coach," I said, then decided I needed to explain myself. "I was just getting some extra shots in—and doing some thinking." I swept my hand in front of me, as if the court were the Grand Canyon or some other inspiring landscape. "Hey, actually," I continued before she could respond, hopping down and walking toward her. "Do you think we could talk?"

All of a sudden I needed to know what it might be like—my new life. I needed to know how to make it work.

"Sure," Coach said. "I have a few minutes."

I followed her down the tunnel, dribbling the ball as we walked. She stopped in front of the coaches' locker room, which I had never entered. She took the keys out of her pocket and opened the door. The space was tiny, so small that you could barely lie on the carpet without pulling your knees in to avoid the stools. There were several lockers, all with clothes hanging from hooks, deodorant on the shelves. Coach Barry grabbed a stool and sat, gesturing for me to do the same. The door clicked shut behind us, leaving just a dim halo of light from the overhead bulb.

"How are you, Kate Fagan?" she asked. Coach Barry often used my full name, I think because she liked the Irish sound of it, our shared heritage. She was perched on her stool, her feet resting on the rungs, her posture ramrod straight, like a good Catholic girl taught by nuns. I was hunched over, elbows on knees, hands cradling my chin, like I was sitting on the end of the bench and didn't expect to go into the game. I answered her by shaking my head, slowly, somberly.

"I know," she said, her eyes softening, and I knew instantly that she did know, probably even more than I imagined she knew. "How are you?" she asked. "Are you hanging in there?"

"I'm not sure that I am," I said. "I'm not sure I know how to hang in like this."

She looked at me sadly, as if she had once said these exact same things to someone else and had sat in the precise spot where I was now sitting. We looked at each other for a moment, then I put an expression on my face that could convey only one request: *Help. Please.*

"What's it like?" I asked her, imagining that she had traveled to the future and somehow made it back to tell us all what was ahead. In reality, this notion wasn't that far off, seeing as she was living my future in a way. I wanted her to share her experience, to show me how I could move forward and still be happy—or, at the very least, not perpetually sad. So she did. She explained her philosophy, and I listened, internalizing every word as if she was giving me the only strategy for survival I would ever receive. Of course, she never suggested I follow the same path (although I would for several years). Things were different for her, she stressed, because she made her living convincing parents, most of them born and raised in the heartland, to let their daughters come play for her. And out lesbians were like the boogeymen of women's sports. She'd had little choice but to pack away this part of herself—this intrinsic piece of her being—stuff it into a suitcase and stash it deep in the closet, unpacking it only on safe occasions, when the people around her would understand all of what was inside.

"Who then?" I asked, tentatively, not wanting to snap this line of communication, to shatter our fledgling trust. "Who gets to know all of you?"

"You'll find those people," she said. "And when you do, keep them close to you." She lifted a hand to her neck, her slim fingers—the ones I had watched a thousand times as she urged us to greatness—resting lightly across her collarbone. "I tell only a select few. I tell only people I absolutely trust. That's it. I'm too worried about the impact on my career."

Years later, a colleague would offer me the most beautiful analogy about the emotional impact of living this way, the pain of living in a glass closet. You tell yourself that you're just wearing a coat, protecting yourself in public, against the elements. You tell yourself it's just temporary, that someday you'll take off the coat and be the real you. But eventually, years later, when the time comes and you're finally ready to shed it forever, you realize you can't.

The coat has become your skin.

CHAPTER 22

Brooklyn Bridge

After my final year at Colorado, I spent a season in Dublin, Ireland, playing professional basketball, then lived in a string of places across the US before settling in Brooklyn. From the spring of 2004, when I left Boulder, until the fall of 2010, I told exactly three people (besides the women I dated) that I was gay: my sister, Ryan; my best friend, Shawna, who I met the year I came back from Dublin, when we played semi-pro ball in Colorado; and Tim, a good friend and colleague at the *Glens Falls Post-Star* in upstate New York. I told Ryan early on, inviting her to an Italian restaurant in Manhattan and setting her up by warning that I had "really awful news," actually hoping she would worry I had an incurable disease, then be relieved to hear what I really had to say. My sister is sweetly non-judgmental, almost laughably so at times, a steadfast believer of "to each his own"—which is to say, I shouldn't have worried, because she has stood by me through everything. I told Shawna within a few weeks of meeting her, sensing that we were in this life together and lying was pointless. It took me more than a year to tell Tim, even though we spent most of each day together, going for long runs and sharing car rides to the newsroom.

My season in Dublin was a complete disaster. In addition to playing for the local team, I also taught basketball at a Catholic school twice a week. But explaining the game to Irish kids was kind of like trying to teach American kids the art of sumo wrestling. It wasn't really part of their culture, so the whole thing was a joke to them, and most lessons ended with the kids kicking the ball back and forth, a much more natural pastime in Ireland. I would shuffle home most afternoons and cry alone in my room; a few times, I actually burst out in tears while still on the school playground, turning around and walking away from the little bastards so they wouldn't see they had conquered me.

Once, on a road trip with my Irish teammates, they got to talking over dinner about how professional women's basketball in the US was filled with lesbians, and I suddenly felt that familiar heat wash over me, the neon sign pointing downward. While in Dublin, I never let anyone know the real me.

And I quit. I left the team midseason. I never thought of myself as a quitter, but that's what I had become. For a few years afterward, my knee-jerk reaction to anything difficult was the desire to stop doing it, to walk away. Quitting is like that: If you open the door even once, you begin looking for the exit in every room you enter.

I've regretted leaving Ireland ever since. I managed to take an awesome, once-in-a-lifetime opportunity and let it morph into a nightmare that I needed to run away from. Every once in a while, I'll imagine how my time in Dublin could have gone better. I picture the lifelong Irish friends I might have bonded with, the trips across the Atlantic to reconnect, the whole experience as rewarding as it should have been.

When I returned home to the States, around Christmas of 2004, I was a mess. I didn't want to keep playing basketball for a living, but I wasn't quite ready to give it up, to return to the bottom of the ladder and begin the climb again, learning an entirely new skill set. So I tried out for the Colorado Chill, a team based in Fort Collins, in the now-defunct National Women's Basketball League. The Chill employed a handful of WNBA players during the winter months (the WNBA runs in the summer), and supplemented the roster with local players, who made significantly less money, sometimes nothing at all, but were at least afforded the opportunity to continue their careers. Meanwhile, I had also begun working part-time for the *Daily Camera* newspaper in Boulder, covering the occasional high school football game.

It was at this crossroads that I met Shawna, who was several years older, married (to a man), and far more settled. The two of us happily rode the end of the bench together, telling jokes, entertaining ourselves by dancing to the arena music during timeouts, and gladly pouring cups of Gatorade for our teammates. Shawna was the first person I was ever completely myself with, constantly disarming me with forecasts of our life-long friendship—the kind of thing that always seemed like total rubbish before I met her. Surely our bond would crumble at some point? Surely I could make it crumble? Instead, Shawna became a steadfast and loyal friend, my sounding board while I tried calming my inner turmoil and irrational fear of rejection.

"Kate, people love you—the real you," she would say. "I promise. You should try trusting them."

I would laugh and say, "You don't know!" But her words meant everything to me, little sips of water as I ran my lonely mental marathon.

Shawna was with me during one Chill road trip when we went to a teammate's hotel room for Bible study. We were curious, but not about Jesus: The woman leading the session was a WNBA star and had a long-term girlfriend whom we had met the previous evening at dinner. At some point during the Bible study, our teammate addressed this issue by explaining that her gayness was temporary, that once her career was over she would find a man and together they would raise a family, as God intended. She would do this, she said, because "being gay is wrong." My eyes flashed to Shawna, a wave of fear rising over me. She shook her head, almost imperceptibly, with a look that said, *Don't listen to this shit; don't internalize it.*

I knew I was done with basketball because I wasn't angry about being stuck on the bench. Clearly, my heart wasn't in it if I was fine shagging rebounds and filling cups of water instead of actually competing for playing time. I had long pictured myself as a writer, ever since reading a story in *Sports Illustrated* about the University of Connecticut women's basketball team and its undefeated run to the 1995 NCAA championship.

I was thirteen at the time, and I remember finishing the story, walking downstairs and showing the magazine to my mom, who was hunched over the sink, her hands immersed in soapy water. "I've decided this is what I'm going to do when I grow up," I told her, pointing to the cover, which featured UConn point guard Jen Rizzotti. "I'm going to be a writer." So in the beginning of 2006, after two winter seasons with the Chill, I applied for every newspaper job in the continental US (or so it seemed), sending out a hundred packages, each containing my resume and clips from the *Daily Camera*. And over the next two years, I would go from the Ellensburg *Daily Record*, which served a small rodeo town about ninety minutes east of Seattle, to the *Glens Fall Post-Star*, a great mid-sized paper only forty-five minutes from where I grew up, to the *Philadelphia Inquirer*.

I found it difficult to feel truly connected to anyone or any certain place, because I revealed so little of myself to those around me. Whereas some people quickly plant roots wherever they go, I was like a backpacker bounding across the surface, my eyes constantly scanning the horizon for where I was heading next. All my colleagues were kind and gracious, introducing me to their partners and children, and yet I could never cross that line with them, always brewing little white lies about how I was spending my time beyond work. The interaction I most regret was with the editor who hired me to the *Daily Record* and took me under his wing, often inviting me home for dinner with him and his wonderful wife. I never even thought of telling him I was gay, deciding instead to give him the Heisman whenever it seemed like any discussion was becoming personal. I'm sure he wouldn't have cared one bit, but I'll never know.

Sometimes I think of all the friendships I could have had if I wasn't so busy running away from intimacy of any kind. I essentially gave people a glossy pamphlet of myself, bullet point info, heavily edited, none of it the kind of stuff that gets to your heart, that makes you care and remember, that makes a relationship worth maintaining over time and across distances. I became so tired of lying, too, and trying to keep track of the half-truths and omissions. My words felt like a ball of yarn that I randomly tossed about, ensnaring everyone in my path.

When I started at the *Inquirer* in 2008, I was assigned to cover the NBA beat. I sat in a meeting room one day, looking out over the paper's sprawling newsroom as my section editor explained how I would be crisscrossing the country, writing about the 76ers over the course of the eighty-two-game regular season. He was clearly selling to me, even though I had already been sold.

"One night you'll be in Los Angeles, the next night Miami; it'll be a great chance to see the country," he said, leaning back in his rolling office chair, tapping a yellow legal pad with his pen. Then he casually added, "You might even meet your future husband on the road."

Here, he leaned forward, dropping his reading glasses to the edge of his nose and peering at me over them. "Are you seeing anyone? Do you have a boyfriend?"

I suddenly felt lightheaded. This awesome gig, my dream job really, was going to be taken from me before I even started, before I even covered a single preseason practice. Truthfully, yes, I was seeing someone, but she was not a boy. (And she was not Ashley; that relationship had ended a year after it began.) My hands were folded on the table, and I moved them underneath me, sitting on them. Then I looked my editor right in the eyes and said, "Nope, not seeing anyone, no boyfriend—just ready to work."

"Probably better that way," he said. "This beat is a real grind."

In the summer of 2010, the *Inquirer* sent me to South Africa to cover soccer's World Cup. It was one of the greatest months of my life, and yet one of my lasting memories from that trip is my feeling of overwhelming panic in the second half of the match between the US and Ghana in the Round of 16. Somehow I was on the hook to give a ride to a fellow sports journalist, someone I barely knew, if the Americans won and sent us both on to the next venue. The thing was, my girlfriend at the time had joined me in South Africa, and I had no clue how I was going to explain her presence to this guy while we were all in the car for three hours. So I found myself desperately rooting for Ghana, as if I had been born and raised there. I remember clenching my fist, hidden underneath the stadium work desk, when Ghana scored in the first extra period, basically sealing my countrymen's fate. The whole moment was wrong, twisted, the opposite of how it should have been, and I had no one to blame but myself.

Even worse than the lying were the walls I built around myself, an invisible fortress to protect me from such scary things as love, trust, intimacy—the emotions that make life so much more rewarding. My heart was starting to shrivel, living as it was in the shadow of those walls.

In the weeks after I returned from the World Cup, I had a meeting at the New York City offices of *ESPN The Magazine* to discuss a story I'd pitched about homophobia in women's college basketball recruiting. I sat with several editors in the corner office that belonged to the magazine's editor in chief, and our conversation was refreshingly freewheeling—by turns serious and hilarious—as I explained the intricacies of the recruiting game. When we were all walking out of the room afterward, one of the executive editors, a woman, turned to a male colleague and made a harmless joke about lesbian stereotypes. Then she quickly turned to me and said with a smile, "Of course, I can say that because I'm gay." By now we were standing in the hallway between offices, a few people still milling about, and without thinking I responded, "And I can laugh about it because I'm gay, too." My heart didn't seize until after I had said it, and even then only for a second, because I realized that nobody cared. They registered the info—*cool*—then moved on with their afternoon. (Little did I know that two years later, this engaging woman, Sue Hovey, would become my girlfriend and partner, so entranced was I by her openness and lack of internal homophobia.)

Sparked by that simple interaction, I gradually started trying on truth and transparency for size, to see how it felt. I texted my cousin Brendan, who was like a younger brother when we were kids. "Hey, I have something to tell you," I wrote, followed a few minutes later by a somewhat lengthy message, carefully typed out on my Blackberry, that culminated with, "I'm gay." I remember staring at my phone, anxious for his response.

"That's cool, cuz. You know how much I love you," Brendan wrote back. "More importantly: When can we hang out?"

I have a large and close-knit extended family, and after coming out to Brendan, I progressively told others, aunts and uncles and cousins, each time feeling a sense of relief because I had missed them so much. I had avoided so many family functions, which to me were just a forum for lying. "Katie, are you seeing anyone?" an aunt would inevitably ask, innocently enough. And what would I say? I played out that scene so many times in my mind that I saw it happening everywhere: near the cooler with beers, by the potluck table with the chips and dip, as we walked to our cars.

I'm still trying to make up for the lost time and connection. For years, my parents and I were caught in an unhealthy feedback loop. I believed they were ashamed that I was gay; they believed I was ashamed I was gay. Neither side was fully wrong, or fully right, but our communication had broken down so much that we didn't know what we didn't know. And even worse, we didn't want to outright ask. I often felt judged in their presence, the air heavy between us. The superficiality of our relationship was unbearable at times, considering how close we had once been and how close they remained with my sister. But we've worked hard to repair things, and we're better today than we've ever been, mostly because we try to talk openly rather than reading meaning into each other's words, suspicious and cynical.

Before my last season on the 76ers beat, in the fall of 2010, I asked my sports editor, Jim Cohen, if we could get lunch together. We always went to Sabrina's, which was down the street from the *Inquirer* building and had delicious sweet potato fries. Jim had taken a chance by hiring me at the age of twenty-six, just two years earlier, and I trusted him implicitly. He often teased me for being hard to read and excessively stoic. "Geez, Fagan," he would say, "I can't even get a smile?"

I couldn't really explain myself at the time, but I knew I wanted to, so I gathered up my courage and met him at Sabrina's one rainy day. I didn't sleep well the night before, busily running my lines in my head like I had an important audition. I had long worried that my career would stall if people found out I was gay, a fear introduced by Coach Barry, who lived in a world where that was a legitimate fear, and stoked by my mother, who at times masked her own sadness about my sexuality by saying, "I don't care at all; I'm just worried it will impact your career."

All of this is to say, telling Jim was a particularly therapeutic step. As we were winding down lunch—I had barely touched my turkey sandwich—I finally tried to say the thing I had come to say. He was eating a bowl of chocolate ice cream and telling one of his quirky stories. After he delivered the punch line, I knew it was time. I leaned forward and sipped my water, then took the straw from my lips and started poking at the melting ice cubes, trying to drown each individual piece as it popped to the surface.

"I wanted to tell you something," I began, keeping my eyes down as my pulse quickened. "I just feel like you should know because

I'm realizing it's an important part of who I am." I paused, then I looked up at him and said, "I'm gay. That's all. That's what I wanted to tell you."

There, I had said it. There was no unsaying it now.

"So?" he said, carving out another spoonful of ice cream and holding it aloft. "I think you're great." Then he put the spoon into his mouth and smiled, although whether the grin was for me or for the ice cream, I don't know.

Over the next two years, I successfully conquered interactions too numerous to list here, and each time I said the words—"I'm gay" or "This is my girlfriend"—I felt a little lighter, the burden a bit easier the more I shared my truth. At first I would have to force the words out of my mouth, like pushing a car uphill, practically sweating from the effort. Now, the thought of lying about who I am makes me feel sick, the same way the truth used to.

—m—

I don't talk to Dee anymore, not really. We maintained a casual friendship for a few years, the kind you might keep with a favorite high school teacher, catching up for coffee once a summer or so, touching upon key milestones but little else. After a while, even this loose connection faded, so utterly revolted was I by the mantra of "Love the sinner, hate the sin." Once, a few years ago, my former teammate Lisa sent me a message on Facebook: "I have just been thinking about you a lot lately and praying for you." It's quite possible she says this to a lot of people, a sentiment equivalent to "Hope all is well" or some other standard closing line, but it sent me into a downward spiral anyway. I bitterly logged off and left my apartment to take a walk and clear my head. I started projecting tone and inflection into Lisa's words. Was it, "Prayin' for ya," all light and fluffy-like? Or was it, "I'm praying for you, sinner," all judge-y and intense?

I never responded.

The last time I spoke with Dee was one bright, crisp afternoon in October 2012. I was living in Brooklyn by then, and I was about to publish a column in *ESPN The Magazine* about how it feels to be a gay athlete. The subject got me thinking: Had Dee's philosophy of "Love the sinner, hate the sin" changed in the decade since we sat in that stairwell? Was it possible to rekindle our friendship, both of us admitting to past wrongs? I called and left a voicemail, asking her to call me back when she could. She texted immediately, saying she would give me a ring in about thirty minutes. As I looked at my phone, a feeling of dread came over me, my heart heavy with anticipation and the fear of rejection.

I clipped the leash to Jaxie, my French bulldog, and said, "You ready for a walk?" She shook with all of her seventeen-pound might, propelling herself forward like a little turbine, then racing to the door as we set out, destination unknown. When Dee finally called, more than forty-five minutes later, Jaxie and I had already walked from Park Slope to the Columbia Street waterfront, and we were right then climbing the steps to the Brooklyn Bridge.

"What's up, Kater?" Dee asked, using my college nickname, which only reinforced for me how long it had been since the last time she had called me that.

"Dee," I said, slowly, drawing it out. "How are you?"

We chitchatted for a few minutes about the obvious things: jobs, homes, current locales. Both of us had moved around a lot after college, so we never knew from one year to the next where the other might be living.

"So," I said to Dee, trying to steer the conversation toward the reason for my call. "I've been thinking a lot lately about our last year together at CU."

"Mmmhmm," she said.

By that time, Jaxie and I were almost halfway across the bridge, suspended over the East River, between Brooklyn and Manhattan, dodging tourists and runners and bikers. The sky was pure blue, cloudless. "I'm writing this column," I said. "It's about the philosophy of 'Love the sinner, hate the sin.' You remember using that, right?"

"Yes . . ." Dee said, the word a question mark, a version of "Go on . . ."

"And it got me thinking that it's been so long since then—a full decade, can you believe it? It seems so long ago and yet, also, not, right? And, anyway, I thought that maybe I should just ask you, just call and ask if you still believed in that, if that was still your philosophy, you know?"

I was taking a circuitous route, wandering, verbally procrastinating. Once I started asking the question, I was acutely aware of being unsure if I actually wanted to hear the answer. Maybe it was better not knowing, always believing that the re-blossoming of our friendship was just around the bend.

"You're asking if I still believe in 'Love the sinner, hate the sin,' right?" she said, clarifying. And I remembered in that instant one of the things I loved about Dee, how she just said what she wanted. It wasn't calculated, wasn't meant to knock me on my heels and gain an edge. She simply liked things to be clear and clean, while I had often preferred muddled, everything open for interpretation, so that later I could mold it to become whatever I wanted.

"Yes, that's what I'm asking," I said, laughing at how quickly she had cut through my weeds. "Also," I continued, following her lead, "I want to know if you still believe that being gay is wrong."

"Ah," she said. "Gotcha. Okay."

I heard her take a deep breath, like she was about to plunge underwater. "Well, the answer to that last part is, yes, my personal relationship with God has led me to the belief that it's wrong, that it's not part of God's plan for us. But, and here's what has changed over the years, I no longer believe that interpretation should be everyone's."

"Right," I said, hoping she would continue.

"I'm much more open now to accepting everyone's faith as their own, no matter what religion or denomination or whatever. I don't see it as black and white, right and wrong, Christianity as the only right choice anymore. I think in college I was just starting to process all of that, but I couldn't put it into action."

"I see," I said. "But just to clarify, you still think being gay is wrong?"

"Wrong? That's too strong of a word."

"Okay," I said, trying again. "What would you say? Just that it's not a part of God's plan?"

"That's how I feel, correct."

Jax and I were at the end of the bridge now, approaching the steps that would spill us into lower Manhattan. Dee and I kept talking, about when we could see each other next, about the possibility of rekindling our friendship, which is what we both said we wanted.

"But you're happy, right?" Dee asked, seemingly apropos of nothing, sandwiched between talk of her odd hours at FedEx, where she worked, and my new job with ESPN.

I thought about it for a few seconds, actually looking up at the sky to see if the same weighty feeling would descend upon me as it had for years, like two hands on my shoulders, pinning me to the ground. I waited, not wanting to speak too early, but all I could sense was a lightness, a clarity that I was being exactly who I was supposed to be.

"I am," I said finally. "Yes."

"I'm glad," she said. And then we made plans to speak the following week. I would call her or she would call me, but we would figure it out—for sure, definitely, because it had been too long and it was so good to catch up. But when we said goodbye, I think we both knew there would be no call the following week, or the week after that.

Some bridges you can't uncross.

Acknowledgments

This book exists because Sue Hovey, my partner, is a very good listener. She makes a practice of noticing, and she noticed what happened to my voice, to my psyche, when I talked about my college years. Without her, this story would remain fragmented inside me. She was the first person to see the value in the telling, and for that I am thankful.

Huge thanks also to my agent, Uwe Stender. He originally loved a different book I had written, a novel, but when I sent him this one, he saw its potential and found a home for it. He is kind and dedicated and passionate, and I am lucky he is willing to represent me.

The folks at Skyhorse Publishing were wonderful, always listening to my input, about anything and everything. My editor, Marianna Dworak, took a chance on this book when I wasn't sure anyone would. She understood my purpose in sharing my story, then encouraged me to tell it the way I wanted and needed.

To my former teammates at the University of Colorado: We were all so young. Maybe some bridges we can't uncross, but perhaps we can build new ones. I hope this book finds you well and thriving.

My respect and admiration for Ceal Barry is deep and unwavering. She is a strong, proud, beautiful woman, and I could not have asked for a better coach. The environment in women's sports can be suffocating for those of us who identify as members of the LGBT community. I wish things were better, and I hope somehow this book can help others who wish to live openly and authentically.

Thank you also to Kris Livingston, Kristen Payne, Kami Carmann, and Tera Bjorklund, some of my other favorite people from my time in Boulder. All of you, at one point or another, said or did something (or many things) that made this journey easier for me.

To my family: I'm not sure "thank you" is enough. I know I'm not easy at times, and I know that not everything I wrote within these pages was easy for you to read. But we have stuck together, grown stronger, and I am forever grateful to have you standing by my side. I love you all. Mom, your zest for life is wonderful and contagious. Dad, you taught me everything you know, and made it fun along the way. Ryan, you are with me always, because you have never made me feel less than equal.

To my best friend, Shawna: We are in this life together, right?

And, finally, to Sue and Jaxie, my two favorite creatures in the world: I love our life, and I look forward to waking up with you every morning. Here's to endless lattes and cuddle sessions.